THE VIENNA POEMS: 1938

GEDICHTE AUS WIEN

Copyright © 2009 by Julie Reichert

All rights reserved. No part of this book may be reproduced or transmitted in any form or by any means, electronic or mechanical, including photocopy, recording, or any information storage and retrieval system, without permission in writing from the publishers.

For permission to make copies of any part of this work, contact: drjulier@comcast.net

ISBN: 1-4392-5733-7

Book design by Sarah McElwain
Cover design by Bill Mohr
Back cover photo by Tim Brittain

First edition

Printed in the United States of America

The Vienna Poems: 1938

Gedichte aus Wien

BY

KURT REICHERT

Translated by Julia Bentley
and
Kurt Reichert & John Kroll

ABOUT THE AUTHOR

Kurt Reichert was born in Karlsbad, Austria, on June 16, 1916. He grew up in Vienna, where, as a young man, he studied directing and acting at the famous Reinhardt Seminar and later worked as an assistant director at the Josefstadt theater until he was forced out by the German Anschluss of March, 1938. He and his parents emigrated to the United States later that year.

Kurt originally intended to pursue his theater career in his new country, but instead became inspired by Roosevelt and the New Deal and entered the field of social work, where he earned his doctorate and had an active career for the next forty years, including a stint as president of the National Association of Social Workers (1962-5). While earning his masters degree at the University of Chicago, he met and married Elizabeth (Betty) Bednasz. Together, Kurt and Betty carried on a personal and professional collaboration that lasted more than sixty years and spanned the country from Chicago, Minneapolis, Albany, Philadelphia, New York City and finally to San Diego, California, where they moved in 1970. In 1981, Kurt retired from the School of Social Work at San Diego State University, where he had served both as dean and a member of the faculty.

Immediately upon his retirement, Kurt returned enthusiastically to the acting career he abruptly had to abandon in Vienna. He appeared at theaters throughout San Diego county, capping his career as the Soothsayer in Shakespeare's *Julius Caesar* at the county's premier theater, the Old Globe. He also performed in several short films, including *Wings* (2005), written and produced by his daughter, Julie, and played a leading role in San Diego's acting community as a board member of the Actors Alliance.

Following the death of his beloved Betty in 2004, Kurt continued to lead an active, engaged life that included performance, travel, and social interactions with a wide group of friends. He spent the last day of his life, May 14, 2006, at the Cajun Gator by the Bay Festival, eating, drinking and enjoying his latest pastime, salsa dancing. He died peacefully later that evening.

Throughout his long life, Kurt maintained his zest for living and a humanistic view of the world that kept him vitally interested in politics, cultural affairs, and what it means to be a human being.

THE TRANSLATIONS

Translation is an art subject to tensions of form versus content, unique idiomatic phrases, differing rhymes, rhythms and dialects. These particular poems contain voices written in highly idiomatic Viennese dialect unique to its time and place. The translators attempted to capture — in a completely different place and era — as much as possible the language, spirit, and flavor of the originals. Because of this, many of the translations do not match the originals line-for line.

Six of the twenty-three poems were translated from German to English by Kurt Reichert and his friend John Kroll (I, IV, XII, XVI, XVII, XXIII). They were initially meant to be performed rather than read on the page, and the translators condensed and rearranged much of the material. The poems translated by Reichert/Kroll are marked in the text with the symbol*. The remaining seventeen poems were translated by Julia Bentley.

THE TRANSLATORS

Julia Bentley is a professional mezzo-soprano widely acclaimed for her work with the difficult 20th-century repertoire. She lived in Austria for five years, and returns often to concertize and visit her in-laws, who gave valuable insight into the fine points of Viennese dialect for these translations.

John Kroll is a writer, editor, and playwright in San Diego. He helped Kurt translate the six poems performed at the Actors Festival, and also served as director for several of Kurt's Actors Festival presentations.

INTRODUCTION

In 1931, Adolf Hitler became Chancellor of Germany. In March, 1938, his army occupied neighboring Austria, which was declared part of Greater Germany. In the intervening years there had been severe economic problems and civil strife in Austria, including an attempted Nazi coup, the murder of the Austrian Chancellor, street fights among political groups, and incidents of mob violence against Jews.

When the German army marched into Vienna, it was greeted jubilantly by much of the population who believed that order had now come to chaos. Swastikas appeared all over the city on buntings and in buttonholes. Within a few days, as Hitler imposed his anti-Jewish sanctions, most Jews lost their work. Many tried to emigrate to other countries, but the world, fearing a massive influx of Jewish refugees, was not very receptive. People stood in endless lines in front of all foreign consulates in an effort to somehow obtain emigration papers. Many were unsuccessful and a few years later perished in the Holocaust.

My father, Kurt Reichert, a young man of twenty-two, quickly lost his job as an assistant stage director at the Josefstadt theater. He and his immediate family were among the lucky ones to get American visas because they had relatives living in the United States. While waiting several months for the emigration papers to come through, Kurt roamed the streets of Vienna on foot and bicycle, talking to people, listening to their stories, and absorbing impressions of all he saw and heard. He transformed these observations about people and events into twenty-three poems and dramatic monologues.

Before leaving Austria, Kurt memorized the poems and destroyed the paper originals in order to avoid their discovery and emigration difficulties at the border. Then, on the ship to America, he wrote them down again, adding a final poem, "To a Human Being," as he headed for his new country.

Kurt hoped to present his work in translation in New York in an accustomed setting: a small cabaret of the kind he knew and had contributed to in pre-Hitler Vienna. But before that could happen, life intervened in a swirl of personal events and decisions, and the poems remained unpublished and unperformed.

Sixty-some years later, another set of circumstances suggested the time was right for a public performance of the poems. By then, Kurt had for many years been working as an actor in the San Diego, California theater community. He translated five of the poems (I, IV, XII, XVI, XVII) and performed them as Springtime: Vienna: 1938 at the San Diego Actors Alliance Festival, in May, 2002.

In 2004, the Max Reinhardt Seminar, Kurt's old theater school, sent him their Seventy-fifth Anniversary Report, which discussed frankly the school's complicity with the Nazis during the German occupation. Kurt was invited to provide his own biography, to publicly read his poems in Vienna, and to participate in related events there. Kurt traveled to Vienna in October, 2005, where he read several of his poems in their original German to a receptive and appreciative audience at the Kulturhaus.

Though he'd visited Vienna several times in the intervening years, this trip to Vienna was a homecoming for Kurt, as a person, an exile, and a Jew. Upon his return to San Diego, he created a public presentation about his experiences that he titled *A Jew's Healing Return to Vienna*, which included his five English-translated poems, as well as a new translation of "To a Human Being" (XXIII). He presented this twice, before his sudden death on May 14, 2006, just shy of his ninetieth birthday.

Two months after Kurt's death, eight San Diego actor friends performed the poems, not exactly in a cabaret, but in an intimate theater at the 2006 San Diego Actors Alliance Festival.

In 1938, Kurt was a young man with a particular fondness for the nineteenth century German romantic poet Heinrich Heine, who wrestled with his Jewish identity, sometimes used his work to criticize the German government, and spent much of his life in exile.

The influences of Heine's lyric style are apparent in some of Kurt's poems, though most were written with dramatic rather than literary intent as he sought to portray the cruelty, fear, and despair that he witnessed.

The poems were written before Kristallnacht and the Holocaust, before the murder of sixty-five thousand Vienna Jews and the expulsion of one-hundred-twenty-five thousand more. Our current reading of the poems contains our hindsight view of those events, and, in Kurt's observations, we see the seeds of the subsequent unspeakable horrors.

Toward the end of his life, Kurt wrote: "More than ever during all these years I am struck by the anonymity of millions of refugees and their persecutors in many cultures and on all continents. To them these poems are dedicated."

Julie Reichert
Albuquerque, New Mexico
Spring 2009

CONTENTS

I.	Voices in Front of the Consulate: A Series of Four Encounters	1
	Vor dem Konsulat	
II.	The Old Man and the Young Man.	11
	Der Alte und der Junge	
III.	Jakob Finkel	23
	Jakob Finkel	
IV.	They Leave the Land	27
	Sie Verlassen das Land	
V.	I Visited Familiar Streets	29
	Über Alte Plätze Wandere Ich	
VI.	Dreams	35
	Träume	
VII.	Ghosts	37
	Gespenster	
VIII.	Crying and Laughing	39
	Weinen und Lachen	
IX.	Behind these Bars	45
	Hinter dem Gitter	
X.	Days Gone By, Leave Me at Last	47
	Vergangene Zeiten, Lasst Mich Los	
XI.	Encounter	51
	Begegnung	
XII.	So Begins the Day	53
	So Beginnt ein Tag	
XIII.	Devil's Dance	55
	Satanstanz	
XIV.	Hope	61
	Hoffnung	
XV.	At the Prater	63
	Im Prater	

XVI.	Reading the Storm Trooper Tabloid 67
	Vor dem Stürmerkasten
XVII.	What I Learned in School Today 73
	Anschlusslektionen
XVIII.	Thoughts of a Viennese Storm Trooper 79
	Gedanken eines Wiener S.A. Mannes
XIX.	At the Tavern 85
	Beim Heurigen
XX.	Corpus Christi Day 93
	Fronleichnamsfest
XXI.	Germania 103
	Germania
XXII.	Debris.. 111
	Trümmer
XXIII.	To a Human Being 117
	An einen Menschen

I.
Vor dem Konsulat

Vor den Konsulaten aller Länder standen lange Schlangen von Wiener jüdischen Familien, die immer wieder versuchten, zu irgend einem Land Einwanderungsbewilligung zu bekommen. Man kam da über Lebensschicksale ins Gespraech.

Ich heisse Kolischer Josef und hab
Einen kleinen Schuhmacherladen.
Mein Vater hat ihn mir vererbt.
Der stand auf den Barrikaden

Als man hier kämpfte für Freiheit und Recht
Im Jahre Achtundvierzig.
Der Vater starb. Und dann kam der Laden
Auf mich im Jahre Neunzig.

Und dann zog ich selber in den Krieg
Und stand gegen den Franzosen.
Die haben mir in einer Nacht
Durchs Handgelenk geschossen.

Die Hand blieb steif, doch bin ich wieder
Auf die Front gegangen.
Nach bösen Kämpfen nahmen uns
Die Russen dann gefangen.

Wir wurden nach Sibirien
Im Jahre siebzehn gefahren.
Ja, damals war ich fünfzig alt,
Vor über zwanzig Jahren.

Dort war's nicht schlecht, doch auch nicht schön,
Ich sehnte mich nach Hause,
Nach meiner Frau und meinem Sohn,
Nach Butterbrot zur Jause.

Wir spielten auf der Balalaika
Wiener Tänze und Lieder.
Da hörten wir etwas von Revolution
Das fuhr uns in die Glieder.

Nach sieben Jahren endlich
Konnten wir entfliehen,
Begannen in einer dunklen Nacht
Heimlich davonzuziehen.

Es war nicht leicht, all die Mühen
Ruhig zu ertragen.
Tausende Meilen haben wir uns
Immer weiter durchgeschlagen.

Oft waren sie hinter uns her. In der Not
Begannen wir zu beten,
Und leider mussten wir auch oft
Arme Soldaten töten.

Durch viele Monate waren wir
Bei armen Juden verborgen.
Die guten Leute bemühten sich
Für uns wie für Kinder zu sorgen.

Den langen Weg bis heim nach Wien
Machten wir in drei Jahren.
Mein Sohn war an der Front gefallen
Das hab ich als erstes erfahren.

I. *
Voices in Front of the Consulate:
A Series of Four Encounters

Long lines of Viennese Jewish families stood in front of the consulates of many countries, trying again and again to get entry visas into any country that would accept them. They started talking about their personal histories.

JOSEF KOLISCHER
My name is Josef Kolischer.
I am a cobbler with a small shop
That my father left me.
Our Family has lived here for generations.

My father fought on the barricades
In the uprisings of 1848
For justice and freedom.
I was a soldier myself in the Great War.

I took a bullet in my wrist,
And when it healed I went back to the front.
The Russians captured us and sent us to Siberia,
We were there for seven years.

I dreamed of Vienna, and butter on my bread.
We played the balalaika and sang songs of home.
Finally we fled the prison camp,
With soldiers after us. Some we had to kill.

We hid in poor Jewish villages.
The people sheltered us as if we were children.
Until our pursuers were gone.
It took us three years to get home.

Ich habe dann als kleiner Schuster
Wieder von Neuem begonnen.
Doch das Wenige, das wir uns ersparten,
Ist in diesen Tagen verronnen.

Und gestern sagt die Frau zu mir,
Wir müssen weiterziehen
Aus dieser Stadt, sagt sie zu mir,
Uns anderswo bemühen.

Gott wird uns helfen, sagte sie,
Auch ohne das Ersparte.
Da steh ich nun seit fünf Uhr Früh
Beim Konsulat und warte.

* * * * * *

Professor Markus heisse ich.
Meine Frau und ich, wir stammen
Aus Deutschland. Sie kennen bestimmt
Aus der Zeitung meinen Namen.

Ich habe viele Jahre lang
Volkswirtschaft getrieben,
Vorträge gehalten und für
Zeitungen geschrieben.

Dann kam der Umschwung vor fünf Jahren
Und ich schien die neuen Herren
Leider durch meine Theorien
Und durch meine Rasse zu stören,

Wurde aber ein ganzes Jahr
Gezwungen, dort zu bleiben.
Und gegen meine Überzeugung
Musste ich weiterschreiben,

Von nationalem Heldentum,
Von Feiern, Siegeszügen.
Kurzum, man zwang mich, unser Volk
Ganz schändlich zu betrügen.

Doch schliesslich fand man einen Ersatz
Guter Gesinnung und Rasse.
Da legte man mir schleunigst nah,
Dass ich das Land verlasse.

Es war nicht leicht, hier neu zu beginnen
Seinen Namen neu zu beweisen.
Und nach einigen Jahren begannen die Herrn,
Wie Sie sehen, mir nachzureisen.

Das heitere Spiel begann von Neuem:
Trotz der geänderten Leitung,
Behielt man mich, da Ersatz noch fehlte
Ein paar Wochen in der Zeitung.

Ich musste über Judenhetzen
Freudeshymnen schreiben
„Die Welt besinnt sich und beginnt
die Juden auszutreiben."

Ich brach zusammen und wurde gekündigt
Mit Recht auf fünf Gehalte.
Es gelang uns in die Schweiz zu kommen,
Doch zu flüchtigem Aufenthalte.

Man liess uns vierzehn Tage dort,
Auch das nur gnadensweise,
Dann schickten sie uns auf die Bahn
„zu schneller Weiterreise."

Nach Frankreich konnten wir überhaupt
Keine Bewilligung kriegen.
Da mussten wir hieher zurück.
Ich fand ein Briefchen liegen

But our struggles hadn't ended.
I reopened my shop,
But times were hard,
And money didn't last.

Then yesterday my wife told me,
"We have to leave this place."
At first her words didn't make sense.
This has always been our home.

"God will provide," my wife believes.
"All will turn out well."
For myself, I am not so sure,
But every morning I come at five o'clock and stand in line.

OTTO MARKUS
My name is Professor Otto Markus.
My wife and I come from Germany.
You may know my name from the papers.
For many years I taught political economy,
Gave public lectures, and wrote newspaper essays.

Then, five years ago, the new regime took over.
My theories and my race disturbed the new masters,
But they forced me to stay on for a year
And to continue to write against my convictions,
Adorning history with battle victories and race-pure heroes.

In short, they forced me to spread lies to the people.
Finally they found a replacement with proper connections and
  race
And asked that I promptly leave the country.
So we came here to Austria,
Trying to rebuild our lives and my career.

Am Schreibtisch, einen lieben Brief
Der im Kurzen davor handelt
Man habe meine Kündigung
„In Entlassung umgewandelt."

So bin ich um mein letztes Geld
Auf schnelle Art gekommen,
Harre jetzt vor dem Konsulat
Der Dinge, die da kommen.

· · · · ·

Ich habe nicht mehr zu berichten
Als mein Mann Ihnen schon erzählte,
Nur dass man mich vor einigen Tagen
Auf offener Strasse stellte.

Ich musste „Jude verrecke" schreien
Und durch einen Pöbelhaufen
Zum allgemeinen Gaudium
Mit blossen Füssen laufen.

· · · · ·

Ich heisse Berta Schwarz, bin Witwe,
Mein Mann ist Agent gewesen,
Vor einigen Jahren sehr krank geworden
Und leider nicht mehr genesen.

Nach seinem Tod war es nicht leicht
Von der kleinen Pension zu leben.
Ich musste unser Pflegekind
Leider ins Armenhaus geben.

Der Kleine war bis vor acht Tagen
Gut dort aufgehoben.
Mir aber hat man die Pension
Seit Wochen schon entzogen.

Sehen Sie, und da hatt ich plötzlich
Allen Mut verloren.
Mir kam von einer Hilfsaktion
Noch irgend was zu Ohren.

Fast hatte ich schon was bekommen,
Da wurden sie gehindert
Uns auszuzahlen und bald darauf
Vollkommen ausgeplündert.

Auch meine arme Schwester ist
Vergeblich bitten gegangen.
Doch alles war nutzlos. Wir wussten einfach
Nichts mehr anzufangen.

Es blieb uns nichts mehr übrig,
Als den Gashahn aufzudrehen.
Wir konnten eben aus dem Dunkel
Keinen Ausweg mehr sehen.

Ich bete, ich wünsche meine
Schwester   soll
Dort oben glücklicher sein.
Es ist schon gut so - hier gabs nichts für sie,
Nein, es ist nichts zu bereuen.

Und doch bin ich froh, dass sie mich fanden
Und wiedererweckten zum Leben,
Weil ich dem Kleinen jetzt helfen kann
Und neue Hoffnung geben.

Es war ein Wunder und der Himmel
Sei dafür gepriesen!
Denn sie haben meinen Jakob
Aus dem Armenhaus gewiesen.

Warum behandeln sie uns denn,
Als wären wir ihre Feinde?
Nach dem Tod meiner Schwester wollte ich fragen
Bei der Kultusgemeinde

Wo sie und zu welcher Zeit
Die Arme denn begraben?
Da sagte die Wache vor der Tür

But as you know, the gentlemen of the master race
Followed us after a few short years,
And for me the old game was played out once again.
They briefly kept me at the paper I was writing for
While they looked for a substitute.

In my articles I had to distort ideas,
Shift arguments, invent evidence,
All to one end: "The world is becoming sane again.
It is wiping out the Jews."
I broke down and was replaced.

My wife and I knew we had to get away.
The Swiss let us in for two weeks only—
A fortnight to find another refuge.
We could not get into France,
It's walls were higher than the Alps.

So we were forced to come back here
And start again. Here we wait
In a line that barely moves
For a future gray and unknown.

BERTA SCHWARZ
My name is Berta Schwarz.
Moses, my husband. He died after many months in pain.
Jakob, our sweet foster child. I had to place him in the
   city orphanage
Because my widow's pension was too small to make ends meet.

And then this tiny pension was no longer given out.
I lost all courage. But then I heard a rumor
About a special charity for needy Jews.
They were about to help me when all their funds were taken
   away.

Dass sie kein Interesse haben
Für jüdische Begräbnisse.
Können Sie denn nicht sehen,
Dass der Laden hier gesperrt ist?
Nun machen Sie, dass Sie gehen!

Da bin ich hinausgegangen
An meines Mannes Grabe,
Erzählte ihm von allem,
das ich hier gesehen habe.

* * * * * *

Wir waren in unserem Armenheim
Vierundsechzig Judenkinder.
Der Herr Präfekt hat uns erzählt,
Juden waren auch die Gründer.

Deswegen kann ich's nicht verstehen
Warum sie's weg genommen.
Ganz plötzlich vor zehn Tagen sind
Zwei Männer hingekommen.

Ich habe gehört, wie sie die Frau
Direktor angeschrien:
Die dreckigen Judenbankert haben
Schleunigst von hier auszuziehen.

Die Frau Direktor fragte sie:
Auch die Wickelkinder, die Kleinen?
Sie sagten ja und sie begann
Ganz fürchterlich zu weinen.

Wir haben dann am nächsten Tag
Das schöne Heim verlassen.
Aber die Kleider und anderen Sachen
Mussten wir dorten lassen.

Ich wollte aus meiner Lade noch
Den schönen Pullover, den roten.
Da kam der eine der beiden Männer
Und hat es mir verboten.

* * * * * *

Ich bin froh, dass ich Dich hier finde,
Ich muss Dir soviel sagen!
Mein Herz ist so voller Gedankenfliege
Es ist kaum mehr zu ertragen.

Du weisst doch, dass ich vor Jahren schon
Medizin hier inskribierte.
Als Mädchen wars zwar nicht immer leicht -
Und dass ich fast fertig studierte.

Mit vielen anderen zusammen haben sie
Mich jetzt rausgeschmissen.
Doch andre Dinge schrecken mich mehr
Und bedrücken mein waches
    Gewissen.

Es ist mir selber noch nicht klar,
Ich kann es nur schwer Dir begründen.
Hast Du nicht auch das Gefühl, als ob
Wir vorm letzten Tage stünden?

Die Menschen sind aus den Fugen
    gekommen.
Die einen rasen und toben -
Die andern sind in Lethargie
Und werden nur geschoben.

Und diese sollten endlich, endlich
Beginnen sich aufzuraffen,
Sie habens in sich. Wenn sie nur wollten,
So könnten sie's schon schaffen.

Muss es denn sein, dass die da
    draussen
Nichts mehr finden, als im Bedauern?
Warum denn stossen die Armen hier
Auf unübersteigbare Mauern?

My sister Anna. How she walked all over town
To find a little aid. It was no use.
The two of us were in despair.
To end it all, we turned the gas valve on.

I pray to God that Heaven for Anna will be a better place,
But I am glad they found me before it was too late
So I can somehow care for little Jakob
Because the orphanage now says they can no longer keep him there.

So then i went to get advice
From the Jewish community agency
How my sister Anna could get properly buried.
A guard was standing at the door.

"There is no information here," he said,
"About Jewish burials or anything else.
You have eyes in your head, so why can't you see
This place has been locked up for good."

I walked way out to the cemetery
And sat down at my Moses' grave.
I prayed with him and told him everything.
He said, "You must try to get away. Go stand in line."

LISL HOFFMANN
I'm happy to see you here.
I have so much to tell you.
My head is full of troubling thoughts.

As you know, I studied to become a doctor.
As a woman, it wasn't easy.
I had nearly finished the course

Warum werden wir in leere Länder
Denn nicht hereingelassen?
Wir würden doch jede Arbeit tun,
Wir würden pflastern die Strassen.

Da wird gefragt: Hast Du Verwandte
Im Land, kannst Du Geld erlegen?
Bei uns dürfen keine Fremden herein
Unsrer Gesetze wegen.

Ich wollte, ich könnte denen da draussen
Beschreiben und erzählen
Wie sie die Menschen hier behandeln,
Sie peinigen und quälen.

Aber auch den Verfolgten bei uns,
Den Alten speziell muss ich sagen:
Lasst doch Euren Kopf nicht hängen,
Ihr steht noch vor besseren Tagen.

Gebt es doch bitte noch nicht auf,
Das letzte bisschen Hoffen!
Muss es denn sein, dass da draussen am Friedhof
So viele Grüber offen?

Nur mit Tatkraft geht es vorwärts,
Niemals aber mit Weinen!
Denkt doch an die Jungen nach Euch!
An Eure Kinder, die Kleinen!

Ich wollte, könnt ich nur aus dem Land,
Was ich hier gesehen, verkünden,
Ich will aber nicht den Hass der Welt
Sondern die Tatkraft erzünden!

Ich will beileibe nicht entfachen
Immer neue Affekte!
O, wenn man endlich, statt niederzureissen,
Die Kunst des Bauens entdeckte.

Ich möchte helfen, Neues zu schaffen,
Ich möchte das Leben studieren -
Um endlich die dummen, schlafenden Menschen
Auf schönere Bahnen zu führen.

Ich möchte nach meinem Ideale
Die neuen Kinder erziehen,
Die nur mehr lernen, sich zu hassen,
Und voreinander fliehen.

Herrgott, könnte ich zu Millionen
Wie zu Dir jetzt sprechen
Hätte ich die Stärke, ihren Starrsinn
Endlich zu zerbrechen.

Aus ihrer Ruhe, ihrer Dumpfheit
Wollte ich sie stören.
Fühlst Du denn nicht auch in Dir
Dieses Zucken und Gären?

When they kicked me out,
Me and many others,
But other things frighten me more.

Humanity seems to be coming apart,
Some constantly hissing and roaring,
The others in a sad state of lethargy.

They have in them the strength to rise;
They could if they wanted—
And I look at the world around.

It is hard to explain—
As if we were entering the last days,
That the graves are giving up their dead.
Do you feel it too?

Why are they keeping us out?
Why will they not let us in?
Their countries are empty.

We would do any work.
We would plaster the streets.
Why do they ask, "Do you have relatives there?
Or money?"

Don't they know what is going on here?
I wish I could tell them.
Oh God, good God,
If I could talk to millions
As I am talking to you.

II.
Der Alte und der Junge

Am Kalenberg und Leopoldsberg in dem schönen Wienerwald hinter der Stadt fand man oft alte Österreicher, die ihre erschütterte Lebensperspektive und ihre Liebe über das Land besprachen. Ich fand da in diesen Tagen den einzigen Platz wo Menschen aller Religionen ohne Misstrauen miteinander bekannt werden konnten.

DER ALTE:
Wie still ist's hier oben über der Stadt!
Ich wollte, ich könnte gegen
Die Grauheit da unten mich wehren und sie
Mit einem Griffe zerfegen!

Als Junger, Starker bin ich oft
Sinnend hier oben gesessen,
-Nach all den verlorenen Jahren hab ich
Schon fast diese Zeiten vergessen.

Ich sah hinunter auf die Länder,
Die da kraftvoll lagen
Und fühlte ihre Melodie
In meinem Herzen schlagen.

Ich sah in einem mächtigen Reich
Viel glückliche Nationen
Durch Frieden und durch Eintracht stark
Nebeneinander wohnen.

Die einen sah ich säen und ernten
Auf weiten ebenen Feldern.
Die anderen sah ich Bäume fällen
In dunkelgrünen Wäldern.

II.
The Old Man and the Young Man

On Kalenberg and Leopoldsberg, two hills in the beautiful Vienna Woods behind the city, I often found old Austrians that were talking about their crushed views on life and their love of their country. In those days it was the only place I found where people of all religions could become acquainted without mistrust.

THE OLD MAN:
How quiet it is above the city!
I wish I could defend myself
From its grime, sweep it clean
With one stroke.

In the full strength of my youth
I would often come here to sit and dream.
After so many lost years, that time
Is hardly even a memory.

I'd gaze down on the countryside
Stretched out in splendor
And feel its melody
Coursing through my heart.

I saw within a mighty realm
Many thriving nations
Strengthened by peace and unity,
Living side by side.

I saw some sowing and reaping
On the wide and even fields;
Others I saw felling trees
In the deep green forests.

Sie flössten die Hözer hinab durch wilde
Flüsse als mutige Fergen
Und pflanzten den Enkeln dann neue Bäume
Auf den uralten Bergen.

Am grossen, blauen Strom dort unten
Sah ich Schiffe voll kostbarer Waren
Über des Reiches Grenzen hinaus
In alle Welten fahren-

Und ich sah, wie die Völker des Reichs ihre Besten
In diese Stadt hersandten,
Damit sie wirken sollten hier
Als der Einheit starke Garanten.

Und ich sah der Völker bunte Trachten
Und hörte ihr Spielen und Singen-
In einer mächtigen Symphonie
Schien alles zusammenzuklingen.

Und ich liebte die Ruhe dieses Reichs,
Die ich auch in mir spürte,
Erlebte angstvoll schaudernd mit,
Wie sich's dann später rührte-

Wie erst das Herz, die Glieder dann
Begannen zu erzittern,
Und wie den Körper jäh zerwühlt
Ein krampfhaftes Erschüttern.

Ich stand hier oben und mir war,
Ich hört die Erde ächzen
Und fühlte nach dem Blut des Leibs
Die Widersacher lechzen.

They'd send the timber down wild rivers,
Courageous ferrymen,
And plant new trees for their grandchildren
On the ancient mountainsides.

Below, on the broad blue river
I saw ships laden with rich wares
Destined for distant ports
Throughout the world—

And I saw how the finest
Were sent from every quarter
Here, to this city,
To serve as unity's certain bond.

And I saw their festive clothes,
Heard their playing and singing;
How it all seemed to rise
In a mighty symphony.

And I loved the peace of this country
Which also lived in me,
And then felt the chill of horror
When it cracked and splintered—

It began in my heart,
Then my limbs felt the tremors,
And sudden convulsions
Wracked my body.

I stood right here, and it seemed
I could hear the earth groan
And I felt my enemy's hunger
For the very blood of my body.

Ich wollte schreien und wollte gegen
Diesen Alb mich wehren-
Doch der Traum war Wirklichkeit.-
Und dann kam das Verheeren-

Und während des alles vernichtenden Kriegs
Trug ich in meinem Innern
Als Waffe gegen alle Gewalten
Ein sehnsuchtsvolles Erinnern.

Doch nach den blutdurchtränkten
Wild zerstörenden Jahren
Wurde es grau. Es kamen Zeiten, die
Noch viel ärger waren.

Und wenn ich dennoch manchmal hoffte,
Bin ich heraufgestiegen.
Doch niemals fand ich mehr mein Bild
Da unten vor mir liegen.

Gewaltsam nahmen sie mir jetzt
Den letzten Hoffnungsschimmer.
Das Reich ist tot, und tot mein Traum.
Verloren nun für immer.

DER JUNGE:
Ich sah es niemals, dieses dein Bild,
Und wollte dennoch ergründen,
Wonach du dich sehntest-ich bin ja dein Sohn,-
Doch konnte ich nichts finden.

Denn wenn ich suchte, waren da
Nur Flecken oder Sprünge,
Und überdies blieb allzuwenig
Zeit für solche Dinge.-

I wanted to scream to ward off
The terrible apparition,
But it was no dream.
Then came the devastation.

During the war's vast obliteration
I carried a dear, desperate memory
As a talisman against every threat.

But after all the blood-soaked years
Of wanton destruction,
Everything dimmed. Then came a time
That was even worse.

And when I sometimes hoped for hope,
I'd climb up to this spot
But I never found my peaceful vista again.

They've stripped me of my heart's last light
With brutal force. That realm is dead,
And that dream, forever lost.

THE YOUNG MAN:
I've never seen that vista, but I've always wished
I could understand what it is you miss.
I am your son, after all—
But there was nothing there.

Wherever I looked, there were
Only stains and cracks,
And besides, there was never time
For these things.

Und ich konnt' auch gar nichts finden,
Denn es waren ja Phantasien!
Dann kamen Freunde, wir begannen
Uns gemeinsam zu bemühen.

Man zeigte uns eines Reiches Bild,
Mächtiger als ich's kannte
Aus deinen Träumen,-eines das
die ganze Welt umspannte.

Die Schleier wollte ich zerreissen,
Dahinter es verborgen.
Doch blieb mir allzuwenig Zeit
In des Alltags drückenden Sorgen.

Dann riefen and're mich, ich sollte
Die Geschicke des uralten,
-Des gelobten Lands der Väter-
Helfen zu gestalten.

Auch dieses konnt' ich nicht ergründen
Hinter Nebelfetzen,
Denn immer wilder, ungestümer
Wurde das tägliche Hetzen-

Und nun ist's eines Hexenkessels
Alles zerstörendes Toben-
Und Freunde, Träume, Bilder sind
In alle Welten zerstoben.

-Und gestern steig' ich hier herauf-
Als es beginnt zu dämmern,
Da plötzlich schlägt in meinen Pulsen
Ein atemberaubendes Hämmern:

And there wasn't even anything there,
Only hollow phantoms.
Then friends came to me, and
We decided to search together.

We were shown the image of a realm
Mightier than I'd ever known
From your dreams; it stretched
Across the world.

I wanted to tear away
The veil that blocked my view
But I had no chance
After the demands of each day.

The others called to me again
It's time to remember that distant place,
The fabled land of our fathers—
And I should help them.

But this too was impossible to grasp
Through the trailing mists
And the daily tasks only grew
More heated and haphazard—

And now they've risen
To a deafening, destructive roar
And friends, dreams, images
Are scattered in the wind.

Yesterday I climbed up here
At twilight, and suddenly
My breathless body shuddered
With a hammering pulse:

Ich fühle in mir und um mich
Zum ersten Mal im Leben
Ein Bild- Wie dieses, dem du dich
So oftmals hingegeben.

Doch furchtbar anders, denn statt Frieden
Spüre ich das Toben.
Und unentrinnbar bin dem Chaos
Schrecklich ich verwoben.

Und Wetter jagen jäh herauf.
Es zittern die uralten
Bäume und sie stöhnen
Unter den Gewalten.

Und Wolken fliehen durch die Nacht
In atemberaubender Schnelle
Und Blitze peitschen in den Himmel
Striemen von leuchtender Helle.

Auch in mir zucken der Vernichtung
Flammende Fanale
Und reissen in mein wehes Herz
Schmerzend tiefe Male.

Und jäh beginnt am Horizont
Ein rotes Licht zu fluten.
In meinem Inner'n schreit es auf:
Die Erde muss verbluten!!

Und immer heftiger glüht es dort,
Wie rote Fackelbrände.
Ist dies der Welten Untergang?
Sind wir denn schon am Ende?

I feel in me, around me,
For the first time, a vision
Like the one you'd described
So often

But terribly different; instead of peace
I feel a thundering, and
The inescapable clutch
Of chaos.

Sudden winds rush upwards;
These old trees
Shudder and moan
At the onslaught.

Clouds flee through the night
So quickly it takes my breath away
Lightening cracks across the sky,
In flashes of violent brilliance.

Inside me, the same
Destructive flares are searing
And tear deep welts
Across my aching heart.

Then a blood-red light streams
Across the horizon;
A voice inside me cries out:
The earth must be bleeding!

The glow is spreading quickly
Like gathering torches.
Is this the apocalypse?
Are we already at the end?

Da steigt der ungeheure Mond
Empor in rotem Scheine-
Ein Krampf durchschüttelt meinen Körper
Befreiend und ich weine.-

Und wie die Stürme, die in mir
Und um mich schrei'n, sich legen,
Steigen neue Kräfte herauf,
Beginnen sich zu regen.-

Mir ist, als würde das Gestirn
Mich immer höher führen,
Und lässt mich seine strahlend helle
Reine Klarheit spüren-

Und mahnt mich an, des grauen Unheils
Stätte zu verlassen-
Und vorwärtszugehen und weiterzusuchen
Auf ebenen, graden Strassen,-

Und ruft mir zu, es muss so sein,
Dass morsche Welten verschwinden,
Und dass es ewiges Schicksal des Menschen ist,
Neue Welten zu finden.-

A ghastly moon is rising
In the scarlet light;
My body shudders free
And I weep.

As the screaming storms within
And without fall silent,
New strength stirs
And ascends.

It seems to me that the heavens
Are leading me upwards,
And share with me
Their gleaming clarity

And encourage me to leave behind
The city's toxic gray, move
Onwards, search further,
On straight, even roads

And call to me: it will always be so,
That rotting worlds must fall away;
And the human lot will always be
To find the next.

III.
Jakob Finkel

Jakob Finkel wird gejagt-
Kriecht noch schnell mit seinem Pinkel
Irgendwo in einen Winkel
Wartet zitternd, bis es tagt.

Und er seufzt in Angst und Wut:
Wofür lass ich mich erschlagen?
Wozu weiter Bürden tragen?
Wozu lebt ein alter Jud?

Abends wünscht er sich den Tod!
Nicht mehr da sein wär gescheiter!
Morgens trägt er hoffend weiter
Denkend an des Herrn Gebot.

Einen Sabbath-Nachmittag
Sitzt er müde, um zu ruhen.
Heute kann er nichts mehr tun
Nach so vieler Müh und Plag.

Plötzlich hört er, wie die Kinder
Auf der Strasse fröhlich singen,
Dass ihm beide Ohren klingen.
schlafen, denkt er, wär gesünder!

Wütend fängt er an, zu brummen,
Weil sie ihn beim Klären stören,
Dann beginnt er zuzuhören,
Endlich sogar, mitzusummen.

Und der alte Jakob lacht-
-So was gab's bisher noch nie!
Weil die kleine Melodie
Ihm jetzt wirklich Freude macht.

III.
Jakob Finkel

Jakob Finkel is the prey—
Scuttles quickly with his sausage
Somewhere where he won't be seen, or
Heard, he hides till break of day.

And he sighs in woeful scorn:
Once again the whipping-boy,
Why is mine the hardest way?
Why was I even born?

In the night he dreams of death!
Better take a length of rope.
But the morning brings new hope
His God demands another breath.

As the Sabbath wends away
He sits motionless, bereft
Of any plan, nothing left
After the struggles of the day.

What's this? A child's ringing voice
Out on the street and yet too near
The singing grates against his ear;
Sleep would be a better choice.

Angry at the children's song
That breaks his evening reverie
He rails at the effrontery
But stopping short, he hums along.

That his features could seem mild
Instead of care-worn, as they ought!
Who would have ever even thought
A song could make him smile.

Ihm, der sonst das lieben flieht,
Der in stetem, dumpfen Schmerz-
Leicht wird ihm das alte Herz
Und er singt sein erstes Lied.

Zaghaft erst und immer stärker
Jauchzt er, lacht und weint zugleich.
Niemals war er noch so reich
Und er sprengt den armen Kerker.

-Folgt dem Sonnenlichte nach
Auf die strahlend grüne Flur,
Sieht des schnellen Hirsches Spur,
und den Fisch im klaren Bach-

Reist durch glühend heisse Wüsten,
Steht dann staunend hoch im Norden
Vor den klaren, kalten Fjorden,
Wandert über Palmenküsten.

Und der riesenhafte Held
Lässt die Stimme machtvoll schallen,
Dass die Felsen widerhallen-
Ihm gehört die ganze Welt!

Als dann nach der Fieberglut
In der Nacht die Kälte kam
Seufzte Jakob voller Gram:
Wozu lebt ein alter Jud??

He, so long from life withdrawn
In relentless, numbing pain
Now hears his heart call out again
And answers with a song.

Halting at first, then holding fast
To every joyous pitch
Never had he felt so rich,
Freed from his bonds at last.

The sunlight's gleaming path he took
On through the verdant grove
He sees where virile stag did move
And fish in brightest brook.

He leaves behind broad burning sands
Arrives astonished in the north
And stands before the bitter fjord,
Sets out to find more tropic lands.

Heroic beyond all human measure,
He sends a mighty ringing tone
That echoes in the halls of stone—
The world is his, and he its creature.

The fevered night is almost gone,
A chill descends on Jakob's brow
In grief and dread he's sighing now
Why was I even born?

IV.
Sie Verlassen das Land

Sie verlassen das Land-
Wohin? Nicht bekannt,
Weil sie nämlich Juden sind!

In die Bücherkiste breitet das Kind
Mit liebender Sorgfalt Zeitungspapier,
Denn die Bücherkiste lassen sie hier.

Weil sie ein Plätzchen erst suchen müssen,
An dem man sie nicht tritt mit Füssen—
Eine selige Insel im Blutmeer der Welt.

Die wenigen Freunde sind heute bestellt
Um ein Lebewohl zu sagen.
Ein „Lebe wohl" in schöneren Tagen.

Tanten bringen Vergissmeinnicht-
-die Guten verstehen das Geschehen noch nicht.
Klügere spenden Körbe mit Essen,

Stumm wird um den Tisch gesessen,
Jemand versucht, Ihnen Mut zu machen,
Später ein and'rer, ein wenig zu lachen.

Einer sagt schliesslich „Auf Wiedersehen",
Die Freunde erheben sich und gehen.
Wir gehen nicht als Freunde, wir gehen als Brüder!

Wo aber und wann sehen wir uns wieder?

IV. *
They Leave the Land

Tomorrow they will leave their native land.
Where to? They're Jews. It can't be planned.
This evening they take final looks.

With old papers a child is wrapping books
And placing them in crates with loving care,
Though they must leave the book crates there

And journey out to find a bit of ground
Where they for once may not be kicked around—
An island in the bloody sea.

The friends they trust come by for bread and tea,
To bid farewell, to wish for better days.
They fill each customary phrase

With feeling. Then some white-haired aunts slip in
And bring forget-me-nots. They can't take in
How all of this has come to pass.

But wisher ones who know too well, alas,
Bring packs of food the wanderers can't take.
They recognize what is at stake.

Then silence, broken by a soft remark,
A word of hope, some laughter in the dark,
Then awkwardly the friends arise

To make—can it be true?—their last goodbyes
With hugs and nods, so they don't have to say,
"Of course we'll meet another day."
Would that it might be, that they would meet again.

But where? And when?

V.
Über Alte Plätze Wandere Ich

Über alte Plätze wanderte ich,
Gedenkend vergangener Ferne-
Du liebe Stadt, wie hatte ich dich
Einstmals doch so gerne!

Wie liebte ich dich als kleiner Bub,
Wenn wir liefen durch deine Strassen,
Und du uns Indianern der Urwald warst
Und wir die Umwelt vergassen!

Wie liebten wir dich, wenn wir eifrigen Knaben
In der Dämmerung spazierten,
über tiefe Wahrheit und über Gott
Und den Teufel philosophierten.

Und wenn uns dann am Weg nach Haus
Die kleine blonde Dicke
An gleicher Stelle jedes Mal
Gewinkt mit ihrem Blicke.

Wie stand ich hinter der Mädchenschule
In zitterndem Hochgefühle,
Bis endlich ein heller Lockenkopf
Erschien in dem bunten Gewühle.

Wie liebte ich Deine Freundlichkeit,
O Wien, Du Stadt der Phäaken,
Deine winkligen Gassen und sogar
Dein Pflaster und deine Laken.-

V.
I Visited Familiar Streets

I visited familiar streets
And thought of times gone by.
You lovely cherished city,
You were once so dear to me.

We mastered all the secret lanes
Where, as Indians, we used to play.
You were our primal forest,
And the world would fade away.

Then in the passion of our youth
And twilight promenades
You heard our debates on deepest truths
And well-worn dieties.

The spot where, on the way back home,
That woman used to stand
To wait for us, with her blonde hair,
All curves and tempting glance.

There's where I stood behind the school
To spy on all the girls,
The one who made me tremble
When she shook her golden curls.

How warmly then you welcomed me,
Vienna, boatmen's home,
I loved your tiny curving streets
And broken cobblestones.

So träumend in schöner Vergangenheit
War ich immer vorwärtsgelaufen,
Da sehe ich plötzlich knapp vor mir
Einen wogenden Menschenhaufen.

Und stehe auch schon eingekeilt
Inmitten der tobenden Meute.
Die lieben Wiener betrachten hier
Frohlockend eine Beute.

Herbei Ihr Leute, kommt und lacht.
Hier gibts etwas zu sehen!
-Ein Wagen, auf dem hoch getürmt
Kisten und Koffer stehen-

Und mitten drauf ein kleines Kind,
Ein Mädchen ganz unschuldig,
Das sitzt auf einem Köfferchen,
Wartet still und geduldig.

Die grossen, schwarzen Augen schauen
Und können nicht begreifen,
Warum die bösen Leute hier
Ununterbrochen keifen.

Du liebes Kleines, ach ich wollt,
Ich könnte Dich entführen
Auf meinen Träumen fort von hier,
Fort von den wilden Tieren.

Fort aus der fremden kalten Stadt,
Aus trüben, grauen Strassen,
Wo alle Menschen leider, dass sie
Menschen sind, vergassen.

Lost in dreams of the golden past
I wandered through the town
Until abruptly I was stopped
Where a surging crowd had grown.

Already I am hemmed in tight
Amid the restless throng;
The citizens are pleased to find
An object for their scorn.

Come gather round! You'll never see
A more amusing view:
A wagon piled with crates and trunks,
Towering and askew.

And just on top a tiny child,
An innocent young maiden
Enthroned upon that suitcase there,
Still and patient, waiting.

Her round dark eyes look out,
So obviously confused
That no one cares to stop the waves
Of laughter and abuse.

You darling child, if only
I could dream you far away
From all these cruel animals
Surrounding you today.

Away from this cold alien place
Of dreary narrow streets,
Where each presents a human face,
Yet harbors such deceit.

O könnten wir zur Sonne
Aus diesem Schatten fliehen!
Dort solltest, kleine Knospe Du,
In Ruhe weiterblühen.

Wir wollen, was wir Böses hier
Gsehen, dann vergessen;
In underem Herzen aber lebt die Heimat,
Die wir einst besessen!

Merk Dir, mein Kind, sie können zwar
Uns schlagen oder quälen!
Eine aber, eines können sie nicht:
Uns unsere Träume stehlen!

If only we could leave behind
The city's shadowed gloom
And seek the sun, you tender bud,
In which you'd thrive and bloom

Then would we gladly cast away
These painful memories;
Within our hearts this place would live
As we would have it be.

So mark it well my child, as hard
And heartless as they seem,
The one thing they can never do
Is take away our dreams.

VI.
Träume

Ich weiss nicht, ob's noch Berge gibt,
Die himmelhoch sich türmen,
Und ob noch Winde heulen und um
Kahle Gipfel stürmen?

Kann man in Schulen immer noch
In engen Bänken sitzen?
Gibts Lehrer? Gibt es Schüler,
Die bei Hausarbeiten schwitzen?

Gibts noch schwarze Abendkleider?
Gibts noch heitere Musik?
Kann man noch im Tanz sich wiegen?
Gibts das noch: ein zarter Blick?

Ist es möglich, dass noch Menschen
Täglich in's Theater gehen?
Und dass andere sich schminken
Und dann auf den Brettern steh'n?

Nein! Dies alles sind gewiss
Bunte Träume nur gewesen!
Oder stand's in einem Buch
Das vor langem ich gelesen!

VI.
Dreams

I don't know if there are mountains
Still towering to the heavens
And if there still are winds that moan
And storm the barren peaks?

Are there still schools, are they still filled
With those narrow benches?
And teachers? Are there students,
Still plagued by long equations?

Is there still formal evening wear?
Is there still lilting music?
Do dancers sway, and is there still
That tender way of looking?

Can it really be, that people still
Buy tickets to a show,
And others who can dress the part
And bow to loud applause?

No, all of these are merely dreams,
A brightly-colored fiction,
Or were written in a book
That I have since forgotten.

VII.
Gespenster

Viele Wochen sind vergangen,
Endlich wieder junge Menschen
    Ebenso wie einst
Zigarettenrauch, Likör,
Weiche, tiefe Armfauteuils
    Ebenso wie einst.

Grammophonmusik, echt englisch,
Willst Du gar nicht mit mir tanzen?
    Nein, ich kanns nicht mehr!
Weisst Du schon das Neueste?
Lach doch auch ein bisschen mit!
    Nein, ich kanns nicht mehr!

Seht ihr nicht die schönen Blumen?
Und das Bild hier an der Wand?
    Waren wir immer so?
Blickt ihr nie aus Eurem Fenster,
Kennt das Leben nicht da draussen?
    Waren wir immer so?

Warum schiesst ihr hin und her?
Tut als wäret ihr berauscht?
    Und ich lache doch!
Leer ist Euer ganzes Tun,
Seid nichts weiter, als Gespenster!
    Und ich lache doch!

VII.
Ghosts

Many weeks have come and gone now,
Finally some younger faces
    Like it was before.
Cigarette smoke, and cocktails,
Armchairs lined with rich upholstery
    Like it was before.

Gramaphone music, how English,
Can't I get one little tango?
    I've forgotten how!
Have you heard the latest joke?
Just pretend to laugh along!
    I've forgotten how!

Don't you see those lovely flowers?
And the painting on the wall?
    Are we still the same?
Won't you look out through your window,
Feel the pulsing life outside?
    Are we still the same?

Why do you fly from place to place
As if you're in a drunken haze?
    I can only laugh!
Every single act is hollow,
You are nothing more than ghosts!
    I can only laugh

VIII.
Weinen und Lachen

Der lachende Neger in diesem and dem naechsten Gedicht ist Erfindung, da es in Wien kaum Neger gab, für mich anscheinlich damals ein Symbol des Triumphs über Nazi Rassenlehren. Vielleicht dachte ich an den Sieg des schwarzen Amerikanischen Boxers Joe Louis im olympischen Boxkampf mit dem Deutschen Max Schmeling.

Wie oft war's, dass ein grosser Schmerz
Mein Inneres zerwühlte,
Wenn ich enttäuscht war, wenn des Lebens
Bitterkeit ich fühlte.

Dann rannte ich durch diese Stadt
Verzweifelt und verlassen
Und suchte Linderung und Trost
In diesen alten Gassen.

Es leuchteten die bunten Dächer
In der Abendröte–
Unendlich zart schien einer schlanken
Kirche Silhouette.

Es lächelte der Abendwind,
Es dufteten die Blumen–
Und es begann das wilde Regen
In mir zu verstummen.

Doch heute find ich keine Ruhe
Auf meinen alten Plätzen,
Ich seh nur grauen, kalten Stein,
Muss immer weiterhetzen.

VIII.
Crying and Laughing

The laughing black man in this and the next poem is an invention, because there were barely any black people in Vienna. For me he was a symbol of triumph over Nazi racial philosophy. Perhaps I thought of the victory of the black American Boxer Joe Louis over the German Max Schmeling in Olympic boxing.

How often a terrible ache
Has troubled my soul
In disappointment,
When I tasted life's bitterness.

Uncertain and alone
I raced through the city
Seeking comfort
In its weathered streets.

The colored roofs glowed
In the sunset, pierced
By the infinite tenderness
Of a church's slender silhouette.

The evening breeze smiles,
The flowers' sweet perfume
Begins to sooth the storm
That raged in me.

But today I can't find peace
In the usual corners;
I see only cold, gray stone,
And stumble on.

Von überall ruft es mir zu:
Da bist ein Paria!
Hast Aussatz, bist ein toller Hund,
Was willst du denn noch da?

Wo ist denn heut, ihr Menschen
Eure rauhe Zärtlichkeit?
Wo ist das kindliche Gemüt?
Ich fürchte, die sind weit.

Seid ihr denn wirklich alle nur mehr
Lumpen und Gelichter?
Und immer wieder prüf ich angstvoll
Jedes der Gesichter.

Da stehen sie wieder und lesen eins
Der niedrig gemeinen Pamphlete!
O, wenn doch einer, wenigstens einer
Etwas wie Abscheu hätte!

Da hör ich plötzlich, wie ein Mann
Vor mir beginnt, zu lachen.
Ein Neger ist's. Was er da sieht,
Scheint ihm viel Spass zu machen.

Er lacht, dass ihm die Tränen rinnen
Von den schwarzen Wangen-
Die Menschen rings umher ergreift
Ein fürchterliches Bangen.

From every quarter
I hear accusations:
"You're a pariah! A rabid dog!
Why are you still here?"

My fellow men, where
Has that natural compassion gone?
The child-like trust?
Far from this place, I fear.

Are you really no more than brutes?
Fearfully I search
And search again
In every countenance.

They gather again to read
One of those awful pamphlets.
If only one of them
Could summon the slightest revulsion!

Suddenly I hear laughter;
The African in front of me
Finds something
Quite amusing.

He laughs till tears
Run down his black cheeks—
The people around us
Shift uneasily.

Er streckt die Zunge weit heraus
Und lacht, und lacht drauf los
Und bleckt die Zähne und mir ist,
Er wächst, wird riesengross.

Die Menschen fliehen, doch er lacht weiter,
Brüllt wie ein Orkan.
O, nimm mich mit, ich lach mit dir,
Hab Dank; du schwarzer Mann!

His tongue extended,
He bares his teeth, and laughs again.
It seems to me
That he grows to a gigantic height.

The people scatter,
And he goes on roaring like a hurricane.
Take me with you, I'll laugh too.
My thanks, you black man.

IX.
Hinter diesem Gitter

Stiller Park, weltabgeschieden,
Zarter, süsser Frühlingsfrieden,
   Hinter diesem Gitter

Bunte Wiesen, reiche Bäume,
Weltendfernte bunte Träume
   Hinter diesem Gitter

Doch in Lettern blutigrot
„Für die Juden hier Verbot"
   Hinter diesem Gitter

Deutsche Menschen, stolz und stumm
Treten in ihr Eigentum
   Hinter diesem Gitter

Und ein Zeichen Deutscher Macht
Ist jetzt alle Blumenpracht
   Hinter diesem Gitter

Und ein Neger, der da geht
Sieht was hier geschrieben steht
   Hinter diesem Gitter

Lacht, lacht für die ganze Erde,
Angstvoll blickt die Menschenherde
   Hinter diesem Gitter

Tiere fletschen ihre Zähne,
Schlange, Marder und Hyäne
   Hinter diesem Gitter

Deutsche Ehre, Deutscher Ruhm,
Ewiges Panoptikum
   Hinter diesem Gitter

IX.
Behind these Bars

Quiet grounds, a world apart,
Tender sweetness, springtime park,
  Behind these bars

Rainbow meadows, arching trees,
Colors only found in dreams
  Behind these bars

Blood-red letters with the news
"No admittance here for Jews"
  Behind these bars

German burghers, smug and worthy
Mutely tour their property
  Behind these bars

One more sign of German glory
This well-kept conservatory
  Behind these bars

There's a black man passing by
Blood-red letters catch his eye
  Behind these bars

He laughs for all the world to hear
Anxious faces turn in fear
  Behind these bars

Flash of bestial tooth is seen,
Weasels, serpents and hyenas
  Behind these bars

German honor, theirs alone,
One low price to see the show
  Behind these bars

X.
Vergang'ne Zeiten, Lasst mich Los

Waldboden, braunes, welkes Laub;
Zerbrochne Äste. Wie die Erde riecht!
Ein Regenwurm, der langsam kriecht
Und Blätter frisst-und alles wird zu Staub

Und Wurzeln krallen sich ins Moos.
Ach, unter diesen Buchen träumt sich's herrlich!
Nein, halt, denn Träume sind gefährlich.
Vergang'ne Zeiten, lasst mich los!

Glitzernd, zart betaute Spinneweben,
Im Winde schaukeln heiter Sonnenblumen,
Die Grillen zirpen und die Bienen summen.
Ewig schillernd buntes Frühlingsleben.

Und der Duft weht her von frischem Heu.
Oftmals machtest du mich trunken!
Nein, nein, alles ist versunken,
Es ist verloren und es ist vorbei.

Ein Dorf mit einem Kirchturm. Frieden. Ruhe.
Ein kleines Häuschen, still und einfach.
Aus Holz die Tische und aus Holz das Dach
Und eine schwergeschnitzte Truhe.

Durch solche Dörfer sind wir oft gegangen,
Als wir... Warum ists denn so schwer
Euch zu vergessen! Es kommt nicht mehr!
Es kommt nicht mehr! Es ist vergangen!

X.
Days Gone By, Leave me at Last

Brown forest floor, decaying leaves lie odorous;
Broken branches. How the soil molders!
An earthworm eating through the older
Foliage—and all returns to dust.

Clinging roots reach through the moss.
Blissful retreat from light of day
Resist! For dreams often betray.
Days gone by, leave me at last.

Glistening webs with dew bedecked,
Proud sunflowers weaving in the breeze,
Chirping crickets, humming bees
The myriad hues of spring's aspect.

How happily I'd once again succumb
Beneath the wafting scent of new-cut hay
But no! All this has fallen away,
All is lost, all is gone.

A church tower in the peaceful town at rest
A tidy cottage, quiet and appealing
All built from wood, from tabletop to ceiling
And a hand-carved wedding chest.

How often we came here with one another
When we… when will this wistful vision
Fade away? Those days are gone!
Those days are gone! All that is over!

Hinweg von hier ich will nichts sehen!
Ich will euch alle nicht mehr grüssen!
O, könnte ich doch meine Augen schliessen
Und als ein Blinder vorwärts gehen.

Schneller, ihr Beine, schneller! Grösseren Schritt!
Klopf nicht; mein Herz, ich bitte, klopfe nicht!
Ich will nicht hören, was das Bächlein spricht,
Nein, Zweiglein, nein, ich nehme dich nicht mit!

Ich will dir nicht den kleinsten Blick vergönnen.
Ich will... Was will ich? Schneller als die Zeit
will ich aus der Vergangenheit
Geradaus in die Zukunft rennen!

I must escape this place, and never find
A shadow of these rural joys,
If only I could close my eyes
And journey on, forever blind.

Faster, my feet, faster, longer strides,
Restrain your surging beat, my heart!
I cannot bring you, willow's slender sprout
Nor linger as the brook confides.

With greater speed than time itself I run
I won't indulge you with the briefest glance
And thoughtlessly forsake the past
Plunging heedless towards what's yet to come.

XI.
Begegnung

Stösst man sich in dunklen Gängen
Wo sich müde Menschen drängen
Jagt nach einem Dokument,
Da geschieht's, dass man erkennt
Eines alten Freundes Blick.

Und man blättert schnell zurück
In des Lebensbuches Seiten:
Ach, wie schön war'n diese Seiten!

„Lang hab ich dich nicht gesehn!—
„Ist dir irgend was gescheh'n??—
„Weisst du denn schon, wann du fährst??—
„Welches Land du dann beehrst??—
„Schreib mir doch mal, wie du lebst!!—
„Ob du Diamanten gräbst!!—
„Hoff, dass wir uns wiedersehn!!—
„Grüss dich, lass dir's recht gut geh'n!!—

Und um ihn nicht zu vergessen
Schreibt man ihn zu den Adressen.

XI.
Encounter

Dark administrative hall
Where too many people stall
In search of one last document
And suddenly one sees a friend
In all the weary pack

Memory's pages turning back
To another time and place:
Hey, weren't those the days!

"I haven't seen you in so long!"
"Tell me what's been going on—"
"Do you know how soon you'll leave?"
"Which lucky country you'll receive?"
"Write to say you're safe and sound!"
"How many diamonds you'll have found!"
"I hope one day we'll meet again—"
"I wish you all the best, my friend!"

And to be sure he won't be missed,
Add one more address to the list.

XII.
So Beginnt ein Tag...

Nach düsterem Traum vergrab ich mich
in meinem Bett und stöhne
Da reissen mich zur Wirklichkeit
Ermunternd falsche Töne.

Was ist's, das mich so rüde weckt?
Sind's Menschen, sind's Gespenster?
In den kalten Morgen starre ich
Erschreckt aus meinem Fenster.

Ach so, wie konnt's ich's nur vergessen:
Wir sind im dritten Reiche.
-Weckruf in aller Herrgottsfrüh-
Das sind die nordischen Bräuche.

Ein müder Blick durch meinen Raum,
Durch die altgewohnten Zimmer,
Es ist, als liege überall
Ein matter, dunkler Schimmer.

Doch seltsam, der Gashahn funktioniert.
Auch rinnt die Wasserleitung-
Und wie gewöhnlich liegt am Platz
Beim Frühstück die Morgenzeitung.-

Der Tee schmeckt schal und in meinem Ohr
Gellt weiter das traurige Klingen,
Begleitet von einem Derwischtanz,
Den die schwarzen Buchstaben springen.

Und die Lettern marschieren in Viererreihen
Hinaus zur Wohnungstüre
Und ich ihnen nach-und plötzlich stehe ich
Vor dem Haus und friere...

XII. *
So Begins the Day

Night. Morning. Which is it?
A nightmare—or not? Am I asleep—or waking?
I hear a groan—perhaps my own.
I burrow into the bed, shaking.

Noise. Joyful? Not really.
From outside—or in? What wakes me so rudely?
Could be a man—or then again
A ghost, whispering lewdly.

Oh, yes, how could I forget?
We are in the Third Reich.
A shock without a warning.
And this is all a wake-up call
To greet the German morning.

Look. My room. Familiar
As always—or not? It's in a haze; it's blurry.
But the heat goes on, the faucets run,
The morning paper appears. Why worry?

And yet—still I hear that noise
Heralding the Third Reich.
Then I pick up the paper.
Its words of rage leap off the page
And dance and mock and caper.

Words—marching—in columns.
They fill up my room. The shriek and spew their venom.
Nazi voices have their stay.
The room, the street, the sun turn gray.
So begins the day.

XIII.
Satanstanz

Ich wandere über Täler und Höhen
Durch's bunte Reich der Träume,
Da tönt eine seltsame Musik
Und füllt die weiten Räume.

Wie tausend Flöten pfeift es schrill,
Dann wieder wird es leise-
Und unergründlich reizt und lockt
Und droht zugleich die Weise.

Und wie mit magischer Gewalt
Scheint es mich anzuziehn-
Ich strebe fort, doch kann ich diesem
Klange nicht entflieh'n.

Und immer schneller treibts mich an,
Beflügelt meine Schritte,
Und plötzlich stehe ich in des weiten
Rathausplatzes Mitte.

Von überall eilen Menschen herbei,
Doch gelähmt von den grausigen Tönen
Mit den starren Gesten hölzerner Puppen,
Doch durchsichtig lautlos, wie Schemen.

Und immer grösser werden die Scharen
Der fahlen, blutleeren Geister,
Es lebt nur einer am ganzen Platz:
Ihr Bändiger und Meister.

XIII.
Devil's Dance

I wander through the realm of dreams
Past cliffs and hidden places
And hear an eerie music rise
And fill the open spaces.

As piercing as a thousand flutes
Then just as quickly fading
A melody strangely ominous
And yet intoxicating

Enmeshed as by a magic force
It seems I'm pulled along
I strain against the bonds, and yet
I can't escape the song.

Still more quickly I am driven
By that piping call
When suddenly I find myself
Before the City Hall.

People disfigured by the spell
Arrive from all directions,
Their gestures wooden as a doll's,
Translucent, silent specters.

Their numbers swell, but in the ranks
Of lurid, bloodless phantoms
Stands only one who is alive;
He owns them, and commands them.

Der Leibhaftige ist's. Hinter Biedermannsmaske
Verbirgt er das Lächeln des Bösen.
Auf seiner riesigen Fahne steht
„Ich mache Geschichte" zu lesen.

Die Flöte setzt er wieder an:
Da dröhnts wie eine Höllen-
Musik und peitscht und zuckt über den Platz
Ein verrücktes, zerreissendes Gellen.

Und es tanzen jauchzend unendliche Scharen
Fanatisch verzückter Gesichter.
Und blutige Fahnen schwingt im Takt
Das menschliche Gelichter.

Und sie legen Leitern am Rathaus an
Und kriechen wie rote Ameisen
Bis auf die Spitze und reissen herab
Den Rathausmann aus Eisen.

Johlende Weiber stecken ihm
Eine Fahne in die Hände
Werfen dann ins ehrwürdige Haus
Lodernde Fackelbrände.

Und die rasende Meute eilt weiter und reisst
Die alten deutschen Denker
Von ihren Postamenten herab
Und die würdigen Schlachtenlenker.

Mit blitzenden braunen Uniformen,
Mit funkelnagelneuen,
Bekleiden Grillpanzer sie und Schiller
Und den Braven Eugen von Savoyen.

He is evil incarnate. A harmless mask
Hides malice and mystery.
A banner displays for all to read:
"I'm making history."

He takes the flute once more and plays
The tune he brought from Hell,
The crowded square convulses
with a wild, ferocious yell.

The twisted faces leap and shout,
A frenzied puppet dance
By endless throngs of people who
Swing countless bloody flags.

Ladders are slung on the City Hall.
They swarm like ants ahead
To the tower, and throw down to the ground
A figure made of lead.

Cackling women squeeze a flag
into his hand, then turning,
they with smoky torches set
the august house to burning.

The mob surges on to dethrone
those honored German sages,
And helpless army generals
Lose their deserved stages.

They unpack brand-new uniforms
Brown in crackling celluloid
To dress Grillparzer and then Schiller,
Noble Eugene from Savoy.

Und wilder wird der satanische Tanz;
Geifernd in wilder Freude
Verbrennen voller Wollust sie
Die alten edlen Gebäude.

Auf fahnengeschmücktem Postament
Steht der Mann und bläst seine Flöte
Und schallend lacht er und freut sich teuflisch
über die flammende Röte.

Und weiter geht der tolle Zug.
Ich sehe noch, wie sie Haydn,
Auch Wagner, Beethoven und Mozart
Mit Stiefeln und Sporen bekleiden.

Und plötzlich wird es still um mich,
Es verklingen die rasenden Stimmen,
Paläste und Kirchen sind niedergebrannt
Die letzten Reste verglimmen.

Auf einem öden, kahlen Feld
Stehe ich ganz alleine.
Einige Raben flattern umher
Mit krächzenden Tönen. - Ich weine.

Grand old buildings are set aflame
By the rabid celebrants.
Insatiable their ruinous lust,
And wilder whirls the devil's dance.

Upon a pedestal bedecked
With stately banners stands the man
And plays his flute, and laughs with glee
As scarlet floods the burning land.

The mad procession marches on
Claiming now those laurelled masters,
Beethoven, Wagner, Haydn, Mozart,
Fitted out in boots and spurs.

Around me falls a sudden hush
As the furious voices die.
Church and palace kneel in ruins,
Embers smolder silently.

On a barren, stony field
The ravens croaking hoarsely kept
Their wary eyes on me, the only
Soul still standing. And I wept.

XIV.
Hoffnung

Isst das Morgen auch schwer für uns
Voll Sorgen und voll Plagen,
Wir haben starke Waffen noch,
Die wir im Herzen Tragen:

Ein starkes Wollen und ein Hoffen
Und ein stilles starkes Versprechen:
Menschen zu sein, wie immer wir leben,
Wir werden es sicher nicht brechen.

XIV.
Hope

If tomorrow proves too heavy,
If we endure the worst,
Know that with these weapons true
Our hearts are reinforced:

Steely desire, and gleaming hope,
A quiet steadfast oath:
Though sorely tried, our human soul
Remains to keep the troth.

XV.
Im Prater

Der Prater ist der bekannte Wiener Vergnügungspark. Der Watschenmann war eine traditionelle Figur im Prater, an der man die Stärke seiner „Watschen", d.h. Ohrfeigen, messen konnte. Die Kommission ist eine Erfindung, die sich daran anlehnte, dass die neuen Behörden in allen Gebieten „rassen-reine" Verordnungen machten, gründlich and mit über-Deutschem Vokabular. Für die Wiener, die seit jeher das „Preussiche" verspotteten, klang das fremd, obzwar leider ein Grossteil der Bevölkerung den Anschluss begrüsste. Für mich wurde nicht nur die neue offizielle Sprache sondern auch der Wiener Dialekt, mit dem ich aufgewachsen war, fremd und hässlich, und ich versuchte, den sprachlichen Kontrast in einigen der Gedichte wiederzuspiegeln.

Der Prater Wien's ist infiziert
Durch Bolschewiken, Judenknechte;
Drum wird er heute inspiziert,
Um herzustellen deutsche Rechte.

Die Kommission marschiert heran:
S.A., S.S., und Kraft durch Freude,
-Jetzt stehen sie bei der Wasserbahn
(Die Ehrendolche in der Scheide).

„Alles freut sich, alles lacht,
Meine Damen und Herrn hereinspaziert!!"
„Otto, hör mal, wat hat er jesacht?
Der doofe Junge hat falsch kommandiert!"

„Kummens, Fräulein, fahrn's mit an Kahn,
Fahrns gradaus ins Schlaraffenland"
-„Hier schreiben wir: Reichsautobahn,
Vergnügungsfahrt zum Reichstagsbrand".

XV.
At the Prater

The Prater was the most famous Viennese amusement park. The Watschenman was a traditional mechanical figure in the Prater, on which you could measure the strength of your 'Watschen' i.e. slaps or punches. The Commission is an invention, inspired by the efforts of the new government departments to make new 'racially pure' laws for all areas of public life that were thorough and written in an exaggerated German diction. For the Viennese, who had always ridiculed the Prussian demeanor, this sounded foreign, even though the majority of the people welcomed the 'Anschluss.' For me, not only the new official language but also the Viennese Dialect, with which I grew up, became foreign and ugly, and I tired to capture the contrast in these dialects in a few of these poems.

With Bolsheviks and filthy Jews
Vienna's Prater Park's infected,
And so to maintain German standards
Now the grounds will be inspected.

Each official brown-clad faction
Marches in to stand beneath
The gilded racks of paddle boats
(daggers mute within their sheaths).

"Ladies and gents, come one, come all!
Step right up! You're livin' large!"
"Otto, I can't believe my ears—
this huckster thinks that he's in charge!"

"Well, little miss, this sweet canoe
will ferry you to Candyland!"
"We'll write instead: enjoy the views
of the burning German Parliament."

Das Ringelspiel dreht sich bis jetzt
Nach Melodien von Offenbach;
Die Deutsche Ehre wird verletzt
Durch diese Wiener Judenschmach"

„Hier spielen wir n'anderes Lied:
Wenns Judenblut vom Messer spritzt,
Das stärkt das kindliche Gemüt,
Und unser Volkstum wird geschützt!-

-Und überhaupt hier diese Hölle
Von janz verschiedener Musik!
Hier sendet die Reichsrundfunkstelle
An jeden Platz det jleiche Stück!!"

Der Watschenmann, der alte brave,
Wird auch in Bälde demoliert:
„Hier kommt n'Maulschellenjudensklave,
Der immer gratis funkioniert."

„Sieh mal, in diesen schäbigen Buden,
Da schossen uns're deutschen Brüder,
Is ne Erfindung von den Juden,
So hielten sie uns ständig nieder."

Mit Tatkraft sie sogleich beschliessen,
Auch hier zu fürdern Mannestugend:
„In Riesenhallen wird hier schiessen
Die treue deutsche Hitlerjugend".

Die Kommission hat inspiziert:
„In die Kasernen, vorwärts, marsch!"
Der Watschenmann denkt resigniert:
„Herr Hauptmann, le.... "

Up to this day the carousel
Played melodies by Offenbach;
Such drivel by Vienna's Jews
Shall no more plague the German folk

"We'd rather hear a different song,
like blood spraying from Jewish necks.
This serenade wins childish hearts
and our proud heritage protects.

The hellish jumble playing here
No cultured ear could long endure;
The national radio will soon provide
The right tune for us all to hear.

The clown-faced punching bag will sigh:
No more tests of strength for me!
"His position will be filled
By worthless Jewish slaves, for free."

"Look at these shabby target shacks
Our German brothers tried to use.
Another attempt to keep us down,
No doubt designed by plotting Jews."

Manly virtue must be supported
A unanimous decision falls:
Our noble German Hitler Youth
Will only shoot in lofty halls.

Smug inspectors leave the park,
Improvement soon will come to pass.
The punching clown thinks to himself
"Your honors, you can kiss my ass."

XVI.
Vor dem Stürmerkasten

„Der Stürmer" war eine Nazi-Zeitung, die als Propaganda überall in der Stadt ausgestellt war.

„Frau Zavertanik!" „Grüss ihnen Gott,
   Freiln Mizzl!,
Ham's schon den Stürmer g'sehn?
Kummen's, les'n's a bissl mit!
Was da Sachen stehn!

Segn's, der Reinhardt hat alle Madln
Auf sein Schloss mitg'nummen
Und hats vergewaltigt! Alle Madln,
Was eam sein unterkummen!

Segns, und da hat ma alleweil
In die Zeitungen g'flesen,
Der Reinhardt und der Toscani sans
so grosse Musiker g'wesen.-

Aber, da steht die Wahrheit jetzt
Von Katzlmachergsindel!
Allweil, wann'd Saujuden kummen sein,
Warns gschreckt, die armen Kindl!

Da steht, man soll seine Kindl
Alles genau beschreiben,
Damit es endlich der Welt gelingt,
Den Teufel auszutreiben!-

Das will ich auch mein Sieglindl erzähln
Sonst tuns ma'fs am End noch
   schänden,
Das G'sindel, was aus Berlin is kummen,
Alle de zugrasten Fremden-

'Hebräischen Emigranten wurde
Unter den Plattfiessen
Im deutschen Reich der Boden zu heiss-
So ham mir leiden miessen!"

„No ja, aber alle warn net a so,
Des muss I ihna scho sagen,
Mei Herrschaft, die kummt a aus
   Berlin,
I kann mi gar net beklagen!

Ausgang hab i alleweil g'habt,
Mehr als gnua zum Essen,
Z'Weihnachten hab i was z'schenken
   kriagt,
Freundlich sans alleweil g'wesen.

Und des muss i ihna a no sagen:
I hab mi schauen mieassen!
Unlängst kummt die Frau Doktor raus,
Des Kleid war ganz zerrissen.

Die is direkt a Greisin wurn,
Die hams auf offener Strassen
Fünf Stunden lang bei derer Költn
Den Dreck aufreiben lassen!"

„Des schad ihr net so viel der Jidin!
Da kann ma gar nix machen!
Glaubens der Hitler selber weiss
Von alle diese Sachen?

XVI. *
Reading the Storm Trooper Tabloid

'Storm Trooper Tabloid' is an attempted translation of 'Der Stürmer,' a Nazi propaganda newspaper that was available all around town in newspaper dispensers.

M Good morning, Frau Zavertanik.

Z How's it going, Mitzi?
Have you read the tabloid here that's just been posted?
Let's see what's going on. Ah, here once more
About that theater director Reinhardt. He should be roasted

Like the pig he is for tempting those sweet Aryan girls
Into his castle. Read the details. You see?
You wouldn't get this in the Jew-run daily press,
But here they tell it all. So juicy.

He has his way with them. Just like a Jew, of course.
One more example of the vermin
Infesting our state. From Berlin, they say.
He thinks, of course, that that makes him a German.

M This family I work for—they come from Berlin.
They're not too bad. I don't have reason
To complain. The food's all right. I get time off
And presents at the Christmas season.

The other day, in fact, I was a bit ashamed.
Frau Doktor staggered home in such condition.
Her dress was torn. They'd made her scrub the street.
It changed her almost beyond recognition.

Alle Leite sagen, in die Wochen
Wär nix gschehn,
Wenn der dagwesen wär in Wien
Und hätt des alles g'sehn.

Des muss a guter Kerl sein,
Der schlagt net amal a Fliegn!
Ich hab in seine Augen s'sehn,
Wie er is ins Auto gstiegn!"

„Mei Herrschaft fahrt natürlich fort
In der übernächsten Wochen,
Weil's es a so behandelt haben!
Was soll i nachher machen?"

„Na, segn's, die Juden tun nur
schaden!
Ihnen tuns entlassen,
Und glaubens Freiln Mizzl, wenn die
  abfahrn
Tuns nix mitgehn lassen?

Die Rojik hat ma erzählt von an
Mann,
Der is nach Frankreich verkummen,
Der hat ihnen, her ich, ganze Sackeln
Mit Goldstickeln mitgenummen!

Na, so an Menschen g'fschiehts schon
  recht,
Wenn er muss Strassen reiben,
Und wenn's nach mir ging, müssten
  alle
Im Lande dahier bleiben."

„Des macht nix aus, Fraus Zavertanik,
I wer a trotzdem entlassen!
Die arischen Madeln mieassen do
Die jüdischen Häuser verlassen!!

I bin von Hand in'd Stadt herein
Und wollt ma was ersparn!
Was bleibt ma jetzt? Der Arbeitsdienst
Oder: heim zur Mutter fahren!"

Z   That's just too bad for her, that Jew.
    If you asked me, she probably provoked it.
    If Hitler had been there himself,
    I'm sure he would have stopped it.

    A month ago when they marched in
    And I was cheering in the crowd,
    I saw him waving from his car.
    He looked quite friendly. Yes, he'll do us proud.

M   Herr Doktor says they'll try to leave.
    They want to go because of their suspicion
    It will get worse for them. But when they're gone,
    My work is gone. What kind of position
    Can I hope to get now?

Z   Mitzi, my dear,
    That's how they work, these saboteurs and traitors.
    You lose your job; they leave with all their wealth.
    They know their tricks, these Hebrew operators.

M   Even if they stayed, I'd have to leave my job.
    You've heard about this latest regulartion.
    We Aryans cannot work for Jews.

Z   And quite right, too. It hurts your reputation.
    To serve the swine. Well, times are hard right now.
    The cost of everything so high. Obtaining
    Milk, even bread, not to mention butter.
    But even so, you don't hear me complaining,

    Although they want to take my boy,
    My only son, and put him in the army.
    Just think of that—and if he has to go to war!
    I must admit, it does alarm me.
    On the other hand, perhaps he'll lose some fat.

„Fräuln Mizzl, machens mich net wild,
Tuns nicht so viel studieren!
Erst gestern hab ich glesen, dass man
Soll nicht kritisieren!

Glaubens, ich bin glicklich iber die
Gemiesepreise heier?
Mehl kann man schon keins mehr kriegen,
Obst ist viel zu teuer!

Und mein Bub muss mit'n Militär
Umeinanderrennen.
Zwei Jahr werns ihm dort behalten,
Hätt was lernen kennen!"

„Na des macht gar nix, höchstens verliert er
Was von seiner Fetten,
Wo kamen ma hin, Frau Zavertanik,
Wann ma kane Soldaten hätten?

Ham se de deutschen Soldaten g'sehn?
Was des für Männer war'n?
Seg'ns, wann i des kunnt, ins Reich hinaus,
Da mecht i glei aussafahrn!"

„Na, ja, fesch schon, aber stellns ihnen vor,
Wenn die in Krieg ziehn missen?
Uns wenn's dann, wie's im Weltkrieg war,
Tausende niederschiessen?

Oder sie missen elendiglich
An an Gasgift ersticken,
Wenns mit die Freimaurer kämpfen müssen,
Mit die Bolschewiken"?

„Gengans, sans gscheit, Fraus Zavertanik,
Sie verstehn nix von de Sachen!
Deutschland muss Soldaten haben!
Wia sollt ma's denn sunst machen,

Dass ma die g'stohlenen Kolonien
Wieder z'fruckakriagn?
Und in die Tschechoslowakei,
Wer sullt denn dorthin ziagn?"

„Na, na, damit is nix, Freiln Mizzl,
Da wern's net einaglassen!
Ja, glauben sie, dass wir uns moechten
Des a so gfallen lassen?

Bei uns, da hat der liebe Hitler
Ganz bestimmt kein Glick.
Adjeh, Freiln Mizzl, G'schamster Diener."
„Heil Hitler, Frau Zavertanik".

M   They are handsome, those young soldiers.
They serve the Fatherland with strength
And joy. How can you hold yours

Back? And soldiers have important work to do.
Our cities are so swollen.
They need to find us living space
And get back our stolen

Colonies. So don't complain about your son.

Z   Or you about that Jewish scum or minor sacrifices.

M   Or you of rising prices.

Z   These changes that we may not like
Increase the glory of the Reich.
Heil Hitler, Mitzi, I must go.

M   Heil Hitler, Frau Zavertanik.

XVII.
Anschlusslektionen

Der zweite Bezirk, Leopoldstadt, war seit vielen Jahren das jüdische Ghetto, wo viele der Einwanderer der letzten Generationen aus östlichen Teilen der alten Monarchie oder anderen östlichen Ländern ansässisch waren, während assimilierte jüdische Familien in anderen Bezirken lebten. Die Sperlgasse war ein Zentrum der Leopoldstadt.

Du, Vater, Du weisst doch, es
   mussten alle
Schüler jüdischer Rasse
Die Schule verlassen und sie kamen
In die Sperlgasse.

Es waere aber doch möglich gewesen
Ihnen Zeit zu lassen!
Sie mussten nämlich in 10 Minuten
Unsere Anstalt verlassen.

Und gestern sagte der Jungvolkführer-
Und das kann ich nicht verstehen-
Wir sollen in die Sperlgasse
Die Juden verprügeln gehen.

Da bin ich mit den anderen
In den zweiten Bezirk gelaufen-
Und unsere Leute begannen dort
Mit den Judenbuben zu raufen.

Dem Pollak habe ich eine geschmiert,
Dem Streber, dem widerlichen.
Siehst du, so habe ich endlich doch
Die alte Rechnung beglichen.

Der kleine Steiner, aber, weisst du,
Der mir die Marken schenkte,
Ich glaube jetzt, was die Leute sagen:
Dass sein Vater sich erhängte.

Der weinte nämlich sehr stark und
   war auch
Ganz schwarz angezogen.
Der Vater muss sicher gestorben sein,
Das war bestimmt nicht erlogen.

Ich hab schon ein bisschen aufgepasst.
Dass sie ihn nicht zuviel schlagen-
Etwas hat er doch abbekommen,
Er wird es bestimmt ertragen.

Ja, Vater, und noch was:
Erinnerst du dich
An die ungeheure Plage,
Die ich mit Mathematik hatte?
Das kommt jetzt nicht mehr in Frage,

XVII. *
What I Learned in School Today

The second district, Leopoldstadt, had been the Jewish Ghetto for many years. Many recent immigrants from the eastern parts of the old Austro-Hungarian monarchy or other eastern countries resided there, while assimilated Jewish families lived in other districts. Sperlgasse was a main road in Leopoldstadt.

Father, the Jew boys in our class
Today received surprising news.
From now on they must go to school
In District 2, with those dirty Eastern Jews.

In minutes, Father, they were ordered out.
I'd walked to school with them this morning.
We'd talked and played and all at once,
They had to leave without a warning.

And later, Father, after school let out,
Our new Hitler Youth leader commanded
Us to go and rough the Jew boys up.
I couldn't understand it.

He ordered, Father, so we all ran down
To pick out some to take a crack at.
Like that fat Pollak, yeah, that's teacher's pet
Was someone I got back at.

But Steiner, Father, he is dressed in black,
So I don't think that folks are lying.
They say his father hanged himself.
Maybe that's why he is always crying.

Denn bei der nächsten Prüfung dürfen
Alle Illegalen
Sich einen Gegenstand erwählen,
Der hat dann auszufallen.

Du, leider wird auch in Geschichte
Ein Grossteil weggestrichen,
Denn unsere Bücher werden alle
Jetzt sehr bald angeglichen.

Der Turnprofessor hat gesagt,
Wir lernen dafür jetzt schiessen,
Und feldmarschmässig wandern,
Und militärisch grüssen.

Denn der Jugendführer meinte,
Das Lernen ist weniger wichtig,
Hauptsache ist, man wird
Im Dienst am Volke tüchtig.

Ja, richtig, gestern im Jungvolkheim
Traf ich den Führer, den neuen!
Ich kenn mich noch nicht aus mit
  ihm,
Er begann sofort zu schreien,

Weil noch nicht alle von uns exakt
Den neuen Stechschritt können.
Wir mussten es gleich am Sportplatz
  üben
Und einige Runden rennen.

Dann war er aber sehr nett und hat
Mit jedem sehr freundlich
  gesprochen.
Und denk dir Vater, er hat mir eine
Uniform versprochen.

Und die Schuhe, die ich requirierte
Bei dem Juden, bei dem alten,
Der dort drüben das Geschäft hat,
Du, die darf ich mir behalten!

Weisst du noch, wie ich bei Kohn
  mit Zement
Die Schlüssellöcher verstopfte?
Und wie ich bei Singer in der Nacht
An die Fensterscheiben klopfte?

Dafür bekomm ich jetzt vielleicht
Das Jugendehrenzeichen.
Der Führer hat versprochen bald
Für mich drum einzureichen!

Aber leider hat er mir verboten,
Das Buch noch weiterzulesen,
Von Tante Anna, die Buddenbrooks,
Bisher wars ganz schön gewesen!

Ja, richtig, wir müssen morgen Früh
In alle Wohnungen laufen,
Und warnen, dass es verboten ist,
Bei Juden einzukaufen.

Und andere sollen zu den Geschäften
Der Juden und warten daneben,
Und wenn jemand trotz des Verbotes
  kauft,
So ist er anzugehen.

Du, Mutter darf nicht mehr zum
  Schuster Kohn,
Das musst du ihr gleich sagen,
Sonst muss ich sie dann übermorgen
Beim Jugendführer verklagen!-

The leader also gave good news for Aryans.
We are allowed to take one subject less.
He said get rid of one you liked the least,
So I picked math, as you can guess.

But as you know, I always liked
What we were taught in Austrian history.
This subject will now be revised
To teach us we belong to Greater Germany.

This leaves us, Father, time that we can use
To practice riflery and drilling
To serve the Reich. The leader says
We'll find it more fulfilling.

This leader, Father, I'm not sure about.
He cursed and then began to scold us.
He yelled because we could not do
The German goose step the way he told us.

We drilled for hours up and down the field
With left foot, right foot, every movement,
But then he promised me a uniform
To reward my great improvement.

He also said the German Reich
Will give us all a badge of honor
For breaking windows in the night
In homes of Jewish pigs like Bronner;

And also for going from door to door
To give a warning to the Aryan neighbors
That they should never buy from Jews
Or give them payment for their labors.

Du denk Dir, wir kriegen Kinokarten
Für eine der nächsten Wochen;
Oder wir dürfen ins Theater,
Das hat er uns versprochen.

Er meinte aber selber, es sei besser
Ins Kino zu gehen.
Da kann man in der Wochenschau
Bilder vom Führer sehen.

Und Samstag bleibt die Schule
    gesperrt.
Denn bei der Grundsteinlegung
Zur neuen Flakkaserne ist
Teilnahme der Jugendbewegung.

Du, ich hab den neuen Führer
Erst nicht leiden könne.
Aber ich glaub, ich werde bald
Mich an ihn gewöhnen.

This means that mother—I now realize it—
No longer should buy shoes from Lehman,
Although she likes his shoes the best.
I'd have no choice but to turn her name in.

Next week we'll go and see a film
And newsreel that the leader says is sure
To show us news of Hitler Youth
And glorious pictures of the Fuhrer.

So Father, altogether we learned a lot today.
Most of it was exciting, some a little sad.
This leader whom I didn't like at first
Will do a lot for us. He isn't bad.

XVIII.
Gedanken eines Wiener S.A. Manns

I wass net, i hab an Angst, die Mizzi
Kennt a Kind von mir kriagn.
Des war a Bledsinn, mit an Bankert
Umananderziaziagn.

Na servas, wann i an Buabn jetzt kriag
Da brauchet i schöne Moneten.
I braucht a Geld, i braucht a paar Schilling,
A paar Mark, wollt i sagn, wann ma hättn.

Was hat der Preuss g'sagt wiar i gestern
Die Unterstützung hab wollen?
Wissen sie nicht, dass sie sich baldigst
Zum Arbeitsdienst melden sollen?"

Des fehlt ma no, i sulltet denen da
Graben ihnere Strassen!
Des Gscheiteste war halt, i mecht mir
Von den Juden ausfüttern lassen!

Des is do net schlecht, was der Franzl derzehlt hat,
Als kommissarischer Leiter
Kriagt der von dem Scjlesinger 1000 Schilling
Und jeden dritten Tag schreit er

Wann er findet, dass was net in Ordnung is
Und der Saujud muass eam zahln.
Der hat ja eh alls was er hat,
Dem deutschen Volke gstohln.

XVIII.
Thoughts of a Viennese Storm Trooper

I don't know. I'm kind of worried
That I got Mitzi pregnant.
How stupid would that be,
To have some brat hanging around?

Hell, having a kid right now
Would take some real money.
I'd need to get my hands on some schillings,
Some marks, I mean.

What was it the Prussian said yesterday,
When I needed a little help?
"Don't you know about the
Volunteer Work Corps?"

That's all I need,
To be out digging streets for them.
If I had any brains, I'd find
Some Jew who needs "protection."

Seems like a good deal, what Franz said;
He gets 1,000 schilling from Schlesinger
to be group leader, raises hell every three days or so
if anything's not right, and the Jew pig pays him.

Whatever he has was stolen from us, anyway.
But it ain't easy to get a job like that, says Franz.
Cause wherever you might find something,
There's always a Prussian waiting to screw you over.

So a Stellung z'kriagn ist aber schwer, sagt der Franzl
Weil de Preissn
überall, wo ma was finden kunnten
Tuans uns einascheissen.

Jede Neubesetzung muss die Führung
Erst gestatten.
Die lebenslänglichen nehmens zerscht
Und die Todeskandidaten.

Was anders ging natirlich a,
Da kunnt i mi schen einhaun,
I kunnt zur Standarte Feldenhalle
Na servas, die Leut täten schauen.

Steht e was drüber in der Zeitung,
Wart amal, wia hasst des -
A da stehts eh, wia s'es nennen
„Verkörperung des Geistes"

Des kling net schlecht und zahln tans a
Und die „Voraussetzungen"?
Als Minestmass für jeden ist
1.70 ausbedungen.

Des bin i ja net. A so a Bledsinn
Na, mir wern schon sehn.
Der Goebbels is no klaner als i.
Des wird schon irgendwie gehn.

In der Uniform schau i grad so aus
Wia alle die Sau-Preussn
A so an Arier bin i no lang!
Ihr werts Euch um mi no reissn!

Every new tour has to go through the same routine.
They take the lifers first,
then the ones who're going to die.

There's other chances too,
I could come out pretty good.
I could get posted to an elite battalion.
Wouldn't that get their attention!

There was something in the paper, too
Wait, what did they call it?
Here it is, something called
"spiritual actualization."

Doesn't sound so bad, and they pay, too.
"Qualifications?" You just have to be
taller than five foot eight. Well,
that's not me. Figures. You never know, though,
Goebbels is even shorter than me. They might
Give me a chance.

In the uniform I look exactly like
Every other bloody Prussian.
I'm Aryan enough all right,
You'll all want a piece of me.

"and also competence in writing skills"—
what idiots. No one'll show.
Okay, anything else in the paper?

„Ferner die durchschnittliche Beherrschung
der Rechtschreibung"-
Die san ja teppert - da kummt ja kaner.
Was steht denn no in der Zeitung?

Der Führer wird die Illegalen
Persönlich dekorieren" -
Was hab i davon? Des Kind von der Mizzi
Muass ja trotzdem krepieren!

Aber fesch wars scho, des muass i sagen
Wia ma no illegal waren -
Wia de Teufeln sa mar in der Nacht
Nach Kärnten aussagfahrn.

De Bruckn san wia Strachhölzeln gflogen
Servas, de san Zersprungen!
Tapfer wars, wia ma am hellichten Tag
Des Horst Wessellied ham g'sungen.

Jetzt hätt i aber gnua vom Singen
A paar Schilling war ma g'sünder.
Halloh, was steht da - schenken sie
Dem Deutschen Reiche Kinder?

Des bin ja i, des tu ma ja!
De werns uns am End no belohnen,
Wann ma dann auf amal mit an
Buam ang'ruckt kummen?

Und sollt des a nix nutzn, fahr i
Nach Australien -
De Juden wern schon wissen, warums
Wegga von da gehn!

"The Führer will personally commend
all illegal residents." So what?
They sure won't be doing Mitzi's kid
Any favors.
But I'd have to say it was pretty fine
When we were still illegal—
How we'd sneak out in the night
And head to the country.

The bridges collapsed like a pile of matches.
Criminy, didn't they just explode!
And it took some guts to sing the Horst Wessel song
In broad daylight.
Now I'd give up singing in a second
For a couple schillings.

Get a load of this!
Make babies for the fatherland!
That's me all over, that's what we're doing!
So you get a prize for showing up with a kid?

And if that doesn't work out either,
I'm bound for Australia.
The Jews aren't leaving town for nothing,
you know.

XIX.
Beim Heurigen

„An dieser Stelle wird wohl altes
Deutsches Brauchtum gepflegt.
Sie wissen nicht, Herr Hinterhuber
Wie mich das erregt.

Ich hoffe, dass es in dieser Weihe-
feierstunde glückt,
Ihnen alles das zu sagen
Was mich so bedrückt."

„Herr Ober, einen Gumpoldskirchner."
„Und ne Portion Klösse.
Ihr Ostmarkdeutschen kennt nicht die
Kulturpolitische Grösse

Zu die uns unser lieber guter
Dr. Goebbels führte.
Wie herrlich war die letzte Rede,
Die ich genau studierte:

Der alte Schutt ist weggeräumt,
Das ist uns nun geglückt,
Und unser Kulturüberschuss,
Der bis jetzt unterdrückt

Wird nun zum kräftigen Einsatz gebracht
Und bestens organisiert
Und unsre Kulturschaffenden,
Die werden diszipliniert.

XIX.
At the Tavern

"This place is consecrated
To hallowed German custom.
Mr. Hinterhuber, I can't begin to tell you
How delighted I am.
I hope to use this precious time
To share what's in my heart."

"Waiter, a glass of your local specialty,
and a portion of dumplings.
You eastern Germans can't conceive
Of the cultural heights to which
Our dear Dr. Goebbels aspires.
His last speech, which I carefully studied,
Was truly inspired:

'The old debris has been cleared away,
A rousing success at last,
And the fruits of our culture,
Which have so long been suppressed,
Will now be fully deployed
And clearly categorized.
Cultural production will receive the benefit
Of discipline.
Our finely-tuned organization
Already boasts functionary conductors
And government poets.'

Es gibt in unserer einheitlichen
Organisation
Ministerialdirigenten,
Reichsfrontdichter schon."

„Ja und Reichsfestpuppenspiele
Des is a schöne Erfindung."
„Richtig, ferner meinte er,
„Die innere Verbindung

Zu den Werten und Inhalten
Deutscher Politik
Muss dem Künstler man vermitteln"
„Sie, des is a Glück."

„Denken sie, der Wolfgang Goethe
Lebte in unsren Tagen,
Und könnte alles sehen, was würde
Der darüber sagen!"

„Der schreibet sicher neue Zitate"
Doch bleiben wir beim Thema,
Wir haben für die Weltgeschichte
Jetzt ein neues Schema.

Man wünscht, dass jeder Deutsche Dichter
Ganz genau erfasse
Historische Personen nach dem
Standpunkt ihrer Rasse."

„Aha, und auch die Musiker, die
Schreiben endlich rassisch.
Herr Schulze, ich muss ihnen sagen,
Ich finde das einfach klassisch."

"Oh yes, and especially those
Nazi puppet theaters, that
Was a brilliant idea!"
"Right, and what's more, he said:
'The intrinsic connection
to the values and goals of the party
must be impressed upon the artists.'"
"Now that's a relief."

"Just imagine if Goethe were alive today,
to witness all this,
what would he have to say!"
"A whole new collection of quotes,
I'm sure."

"But we digress.
 A grand revision will be undertaken.
It is required that all German poets
Take pains to define each historical figure
According to his race."

Aha! And the musicians must finally
show their true colors, too.
Mr. Schulze, I must say
It's not a moment too soon."
"From now on we'll be able to enjoy
a designated culture week
in each district."
"I see! Culture will move on
to a new district every week."
"Hinterhuber, I'm pleased to say
we understand each other perfectly.

„Ferner gibt es jetzt bei uns
Die Gaukulturwoche.
Wir hoffen, damit einzuleiten
Eine gänzlich neue Epoche."

„Aha, die Kultur ist jede Woche
In an andern Gau."
„Ich bin glücklich, Hinterhuber,
Sie verstehen mich so genau.

Und da ich Sie fragen will
Bestärkt mich das jetzt sehr:
Im Namen des Volks, warum sind in Wien
Alle Theater leer?"

„Ach so, Sie sprechen vom Theater"
„Es werden Partei und Staat
Dem Wiener Kulturaufbau helfen,
Wie der Führer verordnet hat."

„Schaun's der Globotschnigg hat gsagt
Die Kunst und diese Sachen
Sind besonders schwer zu behandeln,
Da kann ma halt nix machen!"

„Denken Sie mal gründlich nach:
Fühlten Sie nie ein Streben,
Der Deutschen Kunst sich ganz und gar
Vertrauend hinzugeben?"

Which encourages me to pose this question:
In the name of the people,
Why are the theaters all empty?
The Führer has commanded
The government admistrators
To further Vienna's cultural development."

"As Globotschnigg says,
art and other such things
must be held firmly in check.
There's really no other way."

"Admit it: haven't you felt
that desire to simply
give yourself over completely
to German art?"
"Let's just change the subject, please,
I really couldn't care less
about the theater."

„Gehns, bitt Sie, red ma von was andren,
Des Theater lasst me kalt."
„Ne, mein Lieber, ich lass Sie nicht los,
Es sind nur die Juden schuld:

Hätten die da nicht das Theater verpestet,
So wären sie oftmals gegangen.
Mein Lieber, noch ist's nicht zu spät,
Jetzt darauf anzufangen.

Ich seh's Ihnen an, Sie werden sicher
Noch oft ins Theater gehen,
Sie werden dann die Herrlichkeit
Des Volkstumskampf's verstehen.

Die kulturelle Blüteperiode werden Sie
In sich spüren,
In die unser vielgeliebter Führer
Beginnt zu führen."

„Strengans Ihnen net so an,
Trinkens, wenn es heiss is."
„Prost, mein Guter, so finden wir uns
doch auf gemeinsamer Basis."

„Herr Ober, sagns der Kapelln
I mechts Fiakerlied,
Wissens, des is sehr was Fesch's
Und wirkt auf das Gemüt."

"But that's where you're wrong,
my friend! It's only
because the Jews have corrupted it
that you weren't in the theater every week.
It's not too late for a fresh start;
I can see it in your face:
You'll be there often,
and that's when you'll understand
the triumph of the people
in this cultural battle.
You'll sense the dawn of a golden era
Brought forth by our beloved leader."

"Take it easy now, just have
a nice cool drink."
"Here's to you, brother,
 I couldn't agree with you more."
"Waiter, go tell the bandleader
I'd like the coachman's song.
You'll love this one.
It gets me every time."

XX.
Fronleichmansfest

Das Fronleichnamsfest (Corpus Christi Fest) war eine jahrhunderte alte Tradition, die in allen Stadtteilen mit Prozessionen gefeiert wurde, mit Anteilnahme aller katholischen Vereinigungen, Schulkindern, Feuerwehr, u.s.w. Ich weiss jetzt nicht mehr, welcher Papst Urban mit der Schöpfung dieses Festes zu tun hatte, noch welches der Laterankonzile Massnahmen gegen die Juden beordnet hatte.

Als Papst Urbans ewige Seele
Zog in die Unsterblichkeit
Blickte auf die Erde nieder
Er in Selbstzufriedenheit.

Strich sein Bäuchlein und bedachte
Seines Lebens gute Werke,
Wie der Kirche er gegeben
Neue Kraft und neue Stärke,

Wie der bösen Ketzerei
Machtvoll er begegnet war
Und durch das Fronleichnamsfest
Abgewendet die Gefahr-

-Als das aufgeregte Volk,
 Dirnen warn's und Söldnermassen-
Immer stärker wollten murren,
 Aufruhr war in allen Gassen-

Und am Latorankonzile
Er dies Toben konnt' bezwingen,
Dass die gierig offnen Mäuler
Hallelujah mussten singen-

XX.
Corpus Christi Day

Corpus Christi Day was a centuries-old tradition that was celebrated in all districts of the city with formal parades in which all Catholic associations, school children, the firefighters, etc, participated. I can't recall anymore which pope Urban (there were several popes named Urban) was involved in creating this feast day, nor which of the lateral councils (precursors to the Vatican councils) ordered measures against the Jews in the Middle Ages.

As Pope Urban's immortal soul
Ascended to join the heavenly host
He gazed in great contentment
Upon the earth below.

He stroked his belly and considered
A lifetime of good deeds;
A renewed fortitude bestowed
Upon a church in need.

A fearless confrontation
With darkest heresy
Brought to bear this sacred feast
And turned the threat away—

—as the restless masses churned,
mercenaries, prostitutes
muttered growing discontent
in every narrow street—

His forum the Lateran Council
Heard him thunder and command
Each gaping, ravenous mouth to sing
A halleluia through the land

Denn als guter Hirte liess er
Alle seine grossen Herden
Schon hienieden an des Himmels
Heiligkeit teilhaftig werden.

Wenn er trank von rotem schweren
Gutem sizlianischen Weine,
Dass er sie mit Gottes Leib
Und mit seiner Lieb vereine.

Und er liess die Strassen schmücken
Und mit Gold die Fahnen sticken,
Um durch Pracht und Prozessionen
Seine Schäfchen zu beglücken.

Und um auch die letzte Wut,
Die noch glimmte, zu vermindern,
Bannte er die reichen Juden,
Liess das Volk ein wenig plündern.

Gut, sprach Urban, hab ich das
Wirklich gut hab ichs gemacht.
Dafür, dass mein Vater Schuster,
Hab ichs wirklich weit gebracht.

Und er liess a conto dessen
Sich's recht gut im Himmel gehen.
Blickte immer nur zur Erde,
Seine Prozession zu sehen.

Doch, er wurde immer älter,
Und da er die Gicht schon spürte,
Kams, dass er oft jahrelang
Unten nicht mehr inspizierte.

As shepherd to so vast a flock
He led his charges here below
To ease their aching mortal thirst
Where heavenly waters flow.

And when he too had drunk his fill
Of heavy red Sicilian wine
He felt the melding of his body
And his Master's into one.

Let the streets be decked in grandeur
And the banners sewn in gold,
That my flock may run rejoicing
In processions bright and bold.

And to dampen the last flames
of riot, turn your anger on
these wealthy Jews, and add some plunder
to your celebration.

Fine, he concluded, now that's done.
Really, not too bad a spot.
Now I've arrived, and come so far
From my father's cobbler shop.

Well on these merits he could savor
All the heavenly pleasures there,
And only gaze upon his lambs
On Corpus Christi Day.

But he grew old, and with the gout
It seemed so far to turn
And often centuries would pass
Without the least inspection.

Einst, nach siebenhundert Jahren
Blickte er nach Österreich:
Aber ach, was sieht er da!
Urban wird ganz plötzlich bleich,

Denn sonst schossen die Soldaten
Pöller schon um sechs Uhr Früh.
Heuer jedoch ist es leise,
Aber, ach, wo bleiben sie?

Und sonst prangte doch in Blumen
Und in Reisig jedes Haus!
Heuer jedoch sieht erschreckend
Jammervoll es unten aus.

Nichts sieht er, als Veteranen
In den Prozessionen gehen.
Nichts ist da, als alte Weiber,
Die die Augen fromm verdrehen.

Ach, wo bleiben seiner Jungfrauen
Frischgebügelte Gewänder?
Wo sind ihre keuschen Blicke?
Und die flatternd weissen Bänder?

Wo sind denn die starken Töne
Der freiwilligen Feuerwehr?
Die sonst falsch, doch herzhaft bliesen,
Die vermisst Papst Urban sehr!

Wo bleibt heuer denn die gaffend
Ehrfürchtige Menschenmenge?
Nein, dies ist nicht sein gewohntes,
Leuchtend buntes Schaugedränge!

Once, after seven hundred years
His eye did chance to fall
On Austria, but what was this?
Pope Urban's face grew pale.

Normally the soldiers fire
their salute before the dawn;
Now all around it's strangely silent.
Where could they all have gone?

And the charming houses, once
With flowers and trellises bedecked?
The scene below is quite transformed,
And piteous what is left.

No one else than veterans
To see parading by,
Nothing more than weathered wives
Who turn a judging eye.

Oh! Where are his budding girls
Each in a festive gown?
Where are now their modest glances,
And white ribbons blowing?

Why are there no ringing tones
From the fire brigade
That twisted strident in the air,
Pope Urban's favorite?

Where are the gaping, gawking ranks
He knew so well, that cheered aloud?
No, these here are far removed from
Yesterday's bright colored crowd.

Alles das in Österreich,
Das er immer herzlich liebte?
Das bisher so fromm gewesen
Und ihn niemals noch betrübte?

Urban sinkt in eine Wolke
Ganz verzweifelt und gebrochen.
Lieber Urban, leider hat dich
Ein viel besserer ausgestochen!

Einer, der die Metze Volk
Besser noch, als du, betört,
Und als grosser Zauberkünstler
Schleunigst zum Gebet bekehrt.

Erstens hat er seinem Volk
Brot versprochen und auch Wein-
Und er gibt auch wirklich etwas,
-Denen, die am stärksten schrei'n.

Und den eignen Wein trinkt er
Niemals coram publico.
Er trägt niemals Prachtornate,
Meidet jede Missgunst so.

Und er lässt nicht leise beten,
Sondern laut, in grossen Chören.
Wer nicht betet kann er so
Jederzeit genaustens hören.

Ferner lernte er sehr eifrig
In der Jugend tapezieren-
Prächtiger kann er als Du
Daher Strassen dekorieren.

Everything from Austria
That he had always loved so well,
An idyll long unperturbed,
Far from any trouble?

Urban sinks in swells of cloud,
Rife with doubt, and heavy-hearted.
Dearest Urban, by another
Perpetrator you've been beaten.

A more consummate seducer
Of the people's tawdry hearts
Has woven masterfully the spell
That renders a soul devout.

A bounty of bread and wine
To his acolytes he promised,
And had even more to offer—
To those who cried the loudest.

He never drank his wine in public,
Never wore an ornament.
Doing so would only lead
To envious dissent.

He refused to tolerate
A silent prayer, but rather heard
A roaring chorus, so he'd detect
Precisely who might have demurred.

As a lad he'd proved an apt
Apprentice in wall coverings,
No one will ever gild a street
With such majestic offerings.

Zwingt durch seine Prozessionen
Jedermann, an ihn zu glauben-
Und die Juden darf man jetzt
Bis zum letzten Knopf berauben.

Sag mir Urban, ists ein Wunder,
Dass des Volkes grosse Haufen
Immer mehr sich von dir wenden,
Um dem Adolf zuzulaufen??

Compelled by the beat
Of his parades, every man is certain.
The Jew can finally be robbed
Of his last remaining button.

Confess, Urban, it's no surprise
That mankind's weighty mass
Would turn from you more every day,
To Adolf's shining corpus.

XXI.
Germania

Auf den Bergen, auf den Feldern
Strahlt der Sommersonnenschein,
Vögel zwitschern in den Wäldern,
Blumen blüh'n am Wiesenrain.

Herrlich ist's, weit auszuschreiten
Und in die Natur zu lauschen,
Hier spürt man Unendlichkeiten,
Hier fühlt man des Lebens Rauschen.

Und ich wand're eine Strecke-
Da erklingen starke Töne-
Und es biegen um die Ecke
Scharen deutscher Heldensöhne.

Ach, wie sie die Welt geniessen!-
denk ich mir und geh von hinnen,
Wenn sie mich nur mitzieh'n liessen!
Ach ich wollt, ich könnt mit ihnen!

Sehnsuchtstrunken schreit ich weiter,
Über Täler, über Höhen,-
Da beginnen leise heiter
Milde Lüfte herzuweh'n.

-Milde Lüfte, die sich herrlich
Mit Benzingeruch vermischen,
Panzerautos seh' begehrlich
Ich an mir vorüberwischen.

XXI.
Germania

On the mountains, summer sun
Is beaming, and the meadows
Are ringed with birdsong from the trees
And brightly blooming flowers.

No grander pleasure than to stride,
Attuned to boundless Nature,
With every organ drinking in
Life's infinite elixir.

As I walk along this path
I hear strong, manly tones
And suddenly around the bend
Come Germany's fair sons.

Ah! How they do enjoy this world!
I think as they pass by
If I could only go with them
As far as they'd allow!

With these intoxicating thoughts
I wander up and down the hills—
Then fledgling breezes start to play
From far away in gentle tendrils.

Gentle breezes, subtly mingled
With rich fumes of gasoline.
Armored cars come sweeping by,
I wonder at the changing scene.

Nein!! Ich fühl in mir ein Drängen
Neue Schönheit zu enthüllen!
Möchte alle Berge sprengen,
-Um die Täler auszufüllen.

-Will den Trutz der Felsen brechen
Und dann bauen Autobahnen
Auf den so geschaffnen Flächen-
-Links und Rechts geschmückt mit Fahnen!

Phantasie'n führ'n mich empor
In undenkbar schöne Sphären-
Da tönt etwas an mein Ohr
Und beginnt mich sehr zu stören.

Aber ach! Welch Bild der Wonne!!
Vierzig blonde Mädchenzöpfe,
Heller strahlend als die Sonne,
Und auch zwanzig Speisenäpfe!

Ach! Und wie sie trilirieren,
O, ihr herrlichen Thusnelden,
Ja, ihr seid es, ihr Walküren,
Ihr seid würdig deutscher Helden!

Wie sie sich nur ähnlich seh'n,
Wie gestanzt aus purem Zinn!
Über mich kommt ein Versteh'n
für den neuen deutschen Sinn.

No! This is the end of quiet
Promenades on winding roads,
That nestle on the mountainsides
Like brooklets through the rocky folds.

No! I feel an inner longing
to create beauty anew!
I would blow apart the mountains,
To fill up every valley's trough.

I would break the prideful peaks
And use the newly minted plain
To build highways straight and sleek
Lined with banners in the wind.

My fancy leads me higher, up
To unimaginable spheres.
My reverie is only marred
When unknown sounds assault my ears.

Be still my heart! A glorious vision,
Forty gleaming girlish plaits
Brighter yet than any sun,
And twenty swinging picnic baskets.

Oh! Those voices raised in song,
What rapturous sopranos,
Yes, you Valkuries, you are
Germany's worthy heroes.

How like each other they appear,
As if stamped out of tin!
My eyes are opened, and it's now
I finally comprehend.

Schach dem Individuum,
Das so schlimm es hier getrieben!
Diese Zeiten sind jetzt um!
Nieder mit den Sondertrieben!

Wenn ihr etwas in euch spürt
Einen Drang zum Äpfelstehlen,
Wird auch das organisiert
Nach gemeinsamen Befehlen!

Kampfeseifer uns'rer Jugend
Werden wir gen Feinde lenken!
Werden fürdern Heldentugend,
Mit Granaten euch beschenken!

Und statt Küssen und statt Buhlen
An den Sonn- und Feiertagen,
Werden wir euch schleunigst schulen,
Biologisch Ja-zu-sagen.

Weiter noch geh'n unre Träume,
Denn wir wollen, dass die Eiche
Herrsche über alle Bäume
In dem deutschen Zukunftsreiche!

Ach, es ist nicht auszudenken,
Dass dies alles wird so sein
Und mich drängt's, den Schritt zu lenken
Nach dem kleinen Kirchelein,

Das dor liegt am Hügel droben,
-Dass ich meinen Schöpfer schaue-
Und ihn bitte, den dort oben,
Dass er pfleg die deutschen Gaue

The game is up for the rampant reign
Of individuality!
Those days are finally past!
Down with non-conformity!

If that apple provokes in you
A sudden urge to steal it,
This too has its appointed time
By mutual agreement.

Youth's notorious battle cry
Needs but the slightest guidance,
We'll decorate you with grenades
To honor your defiance.

Waste no breath on words of love.
And wooing every weekend.
Embrace the times, and learn to be
Biologically compliant.

Why stop here? Our dreams include
Tomorrow's wooded slopes
On which it's clear all other trees
Are ruled by mighty oaks.

And yet it's hard to reconcile
This vision of the future,
And lost in thought I find myself
Before a tiny churchyard

Which stands high upon a hill—
The better to see my Maker—
I send a prayer to Him, that he
Should protect each German acre.

Freunde, Freunde, welche Töne
Hör ich da den Chorus singen!
Das Horst-Wessellied, das Schöne
von der Orgel wiederklingen!

Und mir ist, mit einem Mal
Wächst des Kirchleins alt Gemäuer,
-Wird zum Riesendom aus Stahl
Und Beton, ganz ungeheuer-

Und ich seh' auf deutscher Erden,
Wie aus deutscher voller Brust
Deutsche Führer Deutschen Herden
Kommandier'n nach Herzenslust.

Und ich seh' in schwarzen Grüften
Graue Feinde angstvoll schnauben
Während in den Deutschen Lüften
Deutsche Adler hoch sich schrauben.

Und in meinen Visionen
Seh ich durch die Himmelsritzen
Herrlich meinen Führer thronen
Und den lieben Gott dort sitzen.

Wie mir aus der Ewigkeit
Hehre Stimmen so verkünden
Von der Deutschen Herrlichkeit-
Fühl ich meine Sinne schwinden.

My friends, what lovely tones I hear
From this country chorus!
Horst Wessel's song, and mightier still
Its phrases from the organ!

And it seems in one horrid thrust
The church's ancient walls
Rush skyward and are transformed
To concrete domes and steel

And I can hear the German cadence
Proclaimed with passion through this land,
The German herds responding to
Their ruler's every command

And I see in shadowed grottoes
Gray foes panting in despair
While on high the German eagle
Circles upwards in the air

And powerless within my vision
I glimpse through glory-rendered skies
My leader there enthroned majestic
And the Good Lord at his side

In that moment as I hear
Angelic voices raised in praise
Of Germany's exalted state, I
Slip into unconsciousness.

XXII.
Trümmer

I.
Wie ein Alptraum scheint das Leben;
Hinter Nebelfetzen
Seh ich tausend Bilder fliehen,
Schnell vorüberhetzen.

Bilder längst verlor'ner Zeiten,
Zukunftsphantasien-
Plötzlich peitscht die Gegenwart
Und die Bilder fliehen.

Und es drückt aufs müde Herz
Eine Bergeslast-
Aber sinnlos treibts mich weiter
Ohne Ruh' und Rast

Und dann kommen die Gesichter
-Stets sind es die gleichen-
Leidverzerrter, müder Menschen,
Die durch Ämter schleichen.

Möcht mich nur für Augenblicke
Aus der Wirrnis retten-
Und ich flieh zu Schiffahrtsplänen,
Rauche Zigaretten;

Ist dies alles nur ein Traum?
Ach, ich fürchte, nein.
Denn sonst könnte ich doch nicht
Gar so müde sein.

Eins jedoch ist sicher wirklich,
Denn ich seh's vor mir:
Hier mein alter Federstiel
Und dies Blatt Papier.

XXII.
Debris

I.
As a nightmare, life appears
From shrouds of mist uncovered
I see a thousand images
Race by, one after another

Memories of long-lost times,
Dreams of some bright future—
But at the present's rude report
The visions disappear.

And the weight upon my heart
Is heavy as a mountain
But in a weary, senseless blur
I am driven on

Then the faces come again—
always the same ones—
tired people, worn with care
waiting in long lines

Oh, any respite from this daze,
If only a few minutes!
I study cruise ship schedules
And smoke more cigarettes.

Could this all be just a dream?
I cannot answer yes,
For otherwise I'd never feel
This aching weariness.

But still one thing I'm certain of
Because they're simply here:
This, my old familiar quill
And a sheaf of paper.

II.
Oder sind es Geister, die
Alles mir verzerren?
Unterstes nach oben wie im
Zauberspiegel kehren?

Ach ich trüum von fernsten Inseln,
Nichts ist mir zu weit;
Doch mich trennt vom Nachbarland
Eine Ewigkeit.

Und was kostbar war, wird Plunder,
Ach, Du mein Klavier!
Ich wollte, jemand schenkte mir
Ein Paar Schuh dafür!

Und der Polizist dort drüben
Steht ganz plötzlich stramm
Vor 'nem grünen Lausejungen,
Der zu Ehren kam.

Und es müssen alte Lehrer
Exerzieren lernen
Von den eig'nen Schülern und die
Schulen sind Kasernen.

Wirbeln Geister mich umher?
Narret mich ein Troll?
Ach, ich glaube, Geister sind
Nicht so dumm und toll.

Aber in dem wilden Treiben
Bleibt doch etwas mir;
Hier mein alter Federstiel
Und dies Blatt Papier.

II.
Maybe I'm visited by ghosts
That show things at their worst,
Or with a mirror's twisted charm
Display all in reverse?

Oh, I dream of far-off isles
No distance is too far for me;
But the breach between these shores
Is an eternity.

What once was cherished has no worth
And really, what's the use?
I'd gladly give my piano now
For one good pair of shoes!

And that policeman over there
Salutes with quivering respect
Some beardless youth, who has received
The newest commendations yet.

And the elderly professors
Are drilled in formal ranks
By their own pupils, and their schools
are at the army barracks.

Could these be a goblin's tricks?
Are these ghosts that plague me?
There could hardly be, I think,
A spirit that's this crazy.

But amidst all these perversions
Still one thing I can hold dear:
This, my old familiar quill
And a sheaf of paper.

III.
Oder bin ich etwa irr?
Bild mir alles ein?
Und die Wirrnis ringsumher
Ist nur leerer Schein?

Kann das sein?-Da trägt ein Mann
Einen gold'nen Orden,
Den man ihm verliehen hat
für exaktes Morden.

Und ein armer Schlucker ist
Im Kerker jäh verendet-
Gestern Nacht bekam die Frau
Dia Asche zugesendet.

Kann das sein? Zwei Greise mussten
Ihr Geschäft verlassen
Und mit einem Köfferchen
Irr'n sie durch die Strassen.

Einer, den ich wegen seiner
Fröhlichkeit so liebte-
Ist es möglich, dass er Selbstmord
Über Nacht verübte?

Ach, ich fürcht, ich bin nicht irr-
Hab das Parte gelesen,
Und bei seinem Grab bin heut
Am Friedhof ich gewesen.

Aber wenn auch Welten bersten,
Dies gelob' ich Dir:
Meine Feder festzuhalten
Und dies Blatt Papier.

III.
Maybe this is my own madness,
Mere insanity's confusion?
All these chaotic apparitions
Simply a delusion?

Can it be? I see a man
honored with a gold medallion
since he was exemplary
at murder with precision.

Suddenly some poor lost soul
Died in prison like a dog—
And late last night his wife received
His ashes in a box.

Can it be? Two old merchants
thrown out of their workplace
are left to wander through the streets
with nothing but a suitcase.

There's that man who's sparkling humor
Always was a pure delight.
How could it be he'd suddenly
Decide to end his life?

I fear the madness is not mine,
His name was on page five.
Today I visited the church
and stood beside his grave.

But if entire worlds explode
This solemn oath I swear:
I'll keep my old familiar quill
And a sheaf of paper.

XXIII.
An einen Menschen

Mensch, der du deine Ohren
 verschliesst
Gegen fremde Sorgen,
Der du sattgegessen bist,
Heiter und geborgen,

Hör mich an, noch ist es Zeit,
Schnell dich zu besinnen.
Kannst mit deinem Leben noch
Was Besseres beginnen!

Hör, denn deine Brüder leiden
Fern in einem Land.
Bitte hilf!! - sonst sind auf ewig
Dorthin sie verbannt!

Deine Brüder sind gefangen
Und sie leben schlimmer
Als im Kerker, denn sie sind
Ohne Hoffnungsschimmer!

Während du im Bette ruhst
In zufried'nem Schlummer
Wachen deine Brüder und
Weinen dort vor Kummer!

-Schliefen nicht seit Wochen und die
Nerven wollen springen-
Wird der neue Tag wohl wieder
Neue Schrecken bringen?

Während du in schönen Strassen
Dann spazieren gehst-
Und mit frohen Freunden plaudernd
Unter Palmen stehst-

Sehnen sie sich dort nach einem
Hauch von frischer Luft.
Phantasier'n von schönen Ländern

Und von Blumenduft.
Hör, du sollst das nicht vergessen,
Sollst mir Glauben schenken,
Und bei jedem Atemzug
Sollst du daran denken!

Ach, ich seh, das langweilt dich,
Willst nicht weiterhören?
Nein, bleib hier, ich muss dich jetzt
Aus der Ruhe stören!

Während du Zigarren rauchend
Hier im Lehnstuhl ruhst,
Spöttisch überlegen lächelst
Und sonst gar nichts tust-

Wirft man-jetzt!-im Augenblick!
Einen aus dem Zimmer,
Einem schlägt man grad sein bisschen
Hab und Gut in Trümmer!

Wenn dich dann bei deinem Schneider
Modesorgen plagen-
Muss den letzten Rock dort einer
Zum Verkaufen tragen!

Während du dich später mit der
Speisekarte quälst-
Und nach langem Suchen endlich
Roten Wein bestellst-

Warten lange Menschenreihen
Vor einem Asyl-
Warmes Essen zu bekommen-
Meistens ists nicht viel!

Horden kommen dann gelaufen,
Nehmens ihnen weg,
Spucken lachend in den Teller-
Und er liegt im Dreck.

XXIII. *
To a Human Being

You, who closes your eyes against troubles in foreign lands;
You, who are full stomached, happy, and protected.

Listen to me. There is still time to wake up.
You can still do something with your life.
You can begin anew.

Hear me. Your brothers suffer in a faraway land.
They are worse than imprisoned. They have no glimmer of
  hope.

While you stroll under palms, happy with friends,
They yearn for the scent of fresh air.

Listen to me! Believe what I say.
I see this bores you.
You don't want to hear any more.
Oh, no. I have to disturb your peace.

While you smoke cigars, rest in your armchair,
And smile benevolently—

In the same instant, someone is thrown from his room.
His few belongings are broken to bits.

While you are with your tailor, worried about fashion,
Someone has to sell his only coat.

Mensch, du bist noch immer stumm?
Gibts was auf der Welt,
Das dir wert und teuer ist,
Ausser deinem Geld?

Ausser deiner unantastbar
Heiligen Person?
Mensch, sag hast du eine Mutter?
Hast du einen Sohn?

Du, es leben kleine Kinder
Dort in jener Stadt,
Die man aus dem Armenheim
Ausgewiesen hat!

Kinder, du, die lange schon
Nicht mehr froh gemacht,
Werden nie mehr lachen, wird nicht
Hilfe bald gebracht!

Hör mich, während du ein Weib
Kaufst mit einer Kette,
Sie bestichst, damit sie sich
Wälzt mit dir im Bette-

Gibt es Menschen, die sich heimlich
Über Grenzen schleichen,-
Die nicht wissen, ob ihr Ziel
Jemals sie erreichen-

Die nicht wissen, wann die Häscher
Aus dem Dunkel schiessen.
Aber könnten endlich sie
Doch die Freiheit grüssen-

Barfuss, hungernd würden sie
Weinen Freudentränen,
Würden gerne betteln gehen,
So stark ist ihr Sehnen!

Kann dies ungeheure Leid
Dich denn nicht erschrecken?
Kann aus deinem trägen Leben
Dich denn gar nichts wecken?

Gut, schlaf weiter bis zum Tod,
Schlafe nur, du Tier!
Aber wisse, Tausende
Fluchen ewig dir!!

While you devote yourself to selecting
The correct red wine for dinner,
Long rows of people wait to get a little food —
Usually not much.

Are you still silent? Is nothing in the world
Precious and valuable besides your money?
Other than your untouchable holy person?

Tell me, do you have a mother?
Do you have a son?

While you buy a woman,
Bribe her with a gold chain,
So she will roll with you in bed,

There are people who secretly sneak over borders,
Who do not know if they will ever reach their goal,
Who do not know when they will be shot at in the dark.

If they could only at last greet freedom,
Barefoot, hungry, with tears of joy,
They would gladly go beggning,
So strong is their yearning.

Does not their enormous pain frighten you?
Cannot anything wake you from your indolent life?

Good. Then sleep. Sleep unto your death.
But know that thousands curse you forever!

Made in the USA